The man with his gear at Chamonix, 1962. Photo: Ken Wilson.

Rescuers and rescued on the west face of the Petit Dru. Photo: Paris Match.

Gary Hemming

the Beatnik of the Alps

by

Mirella Tenderini

Translated
by

Susan Hodgkiss

 **THE ERNEST PRESS**

Published by The Ernest Press 1995
© Mirella Tenderini 1995

ISBN 0 948153 38 5

British Library Cataloguing-in-Publication Data.
A Catalogue record for this book is available
from the British Library.

Typeset by Askvik Språktjenester A/S
Printed by St Edmundsbury Press

TRANSLATOR'S NOTE

I want to thank Mirella Tenderini for her patient and friendly
cooperation during the translation of her book from Italian.
Also I owe thanks to Lucian Comoy who made many useful
comments on the translation and to Barry Corbet who read the
draft translation and sent constructive criticsm.

Susan Hodgkiss   Hagavik 1995

ACKNOWLEDGEMENTS

Many photographers helped with illustrations for this edition.
Their names appear as photo credits.

CONTENTS

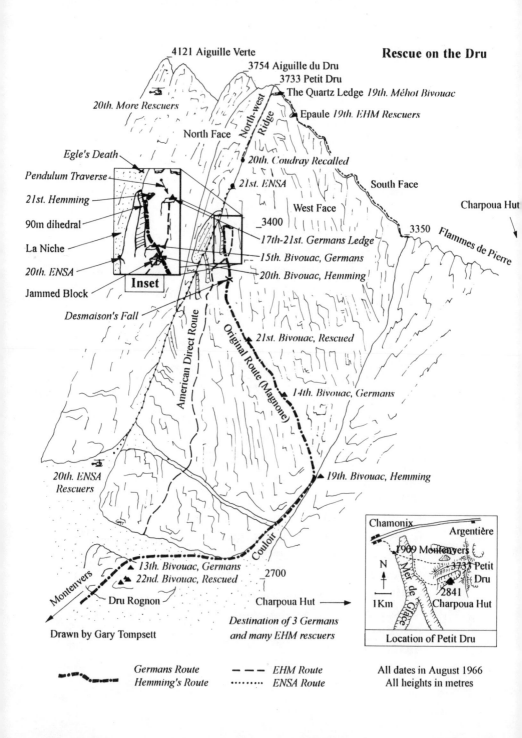

Rescue on the Dru

4121 Aiguille Verte
3754 Aiguille du Dru
3733 Petit Dru
The Quartz Ledge *19th. Méhot Bivouac*
Epaule *19th. EHM Rescuers*
20th. More Rescuers
North Face
North-west Ridge
South Face
Egle's Death
Pendulum Traverse
20th. Coudray Recalled
21st. ENSA
Charpoua Hut
21st. Hemming
West Face
90m dihedral
_3400
3350
Flammes de Pierre
La Niche
17th-21st. Germans Ledge
15th. Bivouac, Germans
20th. ENSA
20th. Bivouac, Hemming
Inset
Jammed Block
Desmaison's Fall
21st. Bivouac, Rescued
American Direct Route
Original Route (Magnone)
14th. Bivouac, Germans
20th. ENSA Rescuers
19th. Bivouac, Hemming
Couloir
Chamonix
Argentière
13th. Bivouac, Germans
1909 Montenvers
N
3733 Petit Dru
22nd. Bivouac, Rescued
_2700
Mer de Glace
Montenvers
Dru Rognon
Charpoua Hut →
1Km
2841
Charpoua Hut
Drawn by Gary Tompsett
Destination of 3 Germans and many EHM rescuers
Location of Petit Dru

●—●—● *Germans Route*   – – – *EHM Route*   All dates in August 1966
•—•—• *Hemming's Route*   ·········· *ENSA Route*   All heights in metres

PART ONE

CHAPTER ONE

Rescue on the Dru

"L'Ecole Militaire de Haute Montagne embarked on a rescue yesterday which is likely to be the most difficult and most dangerous of all rescue operations ever carried out in the Mont Blanc range." [1]

Chamonix, 17th August 1966. The August bank holiday was over, but there were still crowds of holiday makers. Tourists leafing through Le Dauphiné Libéré dwelled on the four column article hungry for details. For some days talk of the rescue had been buzzing round the cafés frequented by mountaineers.

Two Germans had left the village on Saturday August 13th to make an attempt on the west face of the Dru. They bivouacked at the foot of the wall and on the morning of the 14th they began their ascent. The weather was fair, but forecasts warned of worsening conditions.

If you are not a top-class mountaineer and not able

[1] Headlines from Le Dauphiné Libéré August 1966

to move fast up difficult rock, it is always a risk to embark on a long and difficult route at this time of the year. In August, storms in the Western Alps can blow up suddenly and violently. On Saturday the 13th, a hurricane claimed one dead and two wounded in the Vanoise, there were two deaths on the Dent du Géant and two shepherds killed by a bolt of lightning in the Valle d'Aosta.

The German climbers had managed fairly well. On the morning of Monday the 15th they continued to climb, despite the fact that the weather had not cleared completely and it was getting very cold. However, their progress was very slow and that evening they had to bivouac at the foot of the large, 90-metre dihedral.

By Wednesday morning their friends camping at Montenvers were beginning to get worried and asked for help from the Gendarmerie Nationale. The sky cleared for a short while and a helicopter flew over the area. Its pilot was able to make out one of the climbers on a ledge reached after traversing a wall in a pendulum on a fixed rope. The other climber was a few metres below and climbing. They did not seem to be in difficulty and made no signs to the pilot.

That afternoon, during another clear period, their friends spotted them through binoculars from Montenvers. They were still on the same ledge and this time one of them was standing and signalling with some kind of clothing, while the other remained seated and seemed to be exhausted or possibly injured. From their position, a retreat would be difficult: they would have to pull themselves up the rope they had used for the pendulum traverse, hanging over a large void. Above them, cracks leading to large overhangs were full of ice.

Next day, and still they had not moved. By this time their friends were sure that one of them was injured and decided to take some action. The Ecole Militaire de Haute Montagne (E.H.M.) had already organised a group, and by Thursday August 18th a major rescue operation had begun. On Thursday three German climbers set off from the campsite at Montenvers for the Charpoua Hut. They hoped to reach the summit from the hut then abseil down the north-west ridge to the ledge where the two climbers were. An alternative plan was to climb up the north wall to a snow-field called 'La Niche', and from there attempt to reach the ledge by means of a rather precarious traverse. Those in charge of the E.H.M. were determinedly aiming for the summit and then a descent to the unfortunate climbers. A group of guides was making its way to set up camp on the 'Epaule', a 3500-metre-high shelf on the spur of the Flammes de Pierre. In addition, a large group of officers and N.C.O.s, students of the specialised course with the E.H.M. set up camp at the Charpoua Hut, ready to come to their assistance.

Once again, the weather showed signs of deteriorating.

"The two German climbers are still stuck on the west face of the Dru. Snow and strong winds have halted all rescue teams now bivouacked on the summit."

On August 19th it snowed steadily from 17.00 hrs. Sixteen men from the E.H.M. had reached the Epaule. In normal conditions one would be able to see climbers on the west face from this position, but snow and mist had decreased visibility considerably and they were not able to glean any information on the condition of the two Germans. Méhot, the guide from the E.H.M., and three trainee guides tried to make for the summit of the Petit Dru by the normal route, the south face. By 20.00 hrs. they reached *The Quartz Ledge*, approximately 50 metres below the summit, and were forced to spend the night there.

Colonel Gonet, leader of the E.H.M. and head of the rescue operation, had set up headquarters at the Charpoua Hut. Charles Germain, the head instructor of the E.H.M., was ready to start. But for the moment, there was nothing anyone could do.

How would the two Germans be getting on? Would they still be alive? Their friends had reported that they had enough food for three days, and this was their eighth day on the mountain. They had bivouacked on the face for seven nights in extremely low temperatures. They would be thirsty. Even with all that snow and ice around them, they would not be able to get enough water. Were they injured?

A helicopter pilot managed to fly over them early that morning and spotted them. They were moving; they were still alive.

Despite the poor weather the rescue attempt continued. There were now dozens of people involved in the attempt to reach the summit. The four guides who had bivouacked on *The Quartz Ledge* attempted a traverse of the west face towards the north-west ridge. The rock was covered with a thick layer of snow and ice, coating the infrequent holds and making it almost impossible to install the fixed ropes intended to help reinforcements or allow an easy retreat in case the weather deteriorated. Despite conditions, Méhot was optimistic and announced on his radio, "We will reach them this afternoon".

However, it began immediately to snow again. "We can't see a thing, we have to stop." Méhot hoped to start again as soon as the snow stopped but had used all their ropes to secure the traverse. If reinforcements did not arrive with more gear, they would not have enough rope to secure the descent from the ridge, if they ever reached it. He called on the radio, "Come up. We need more ropes, hurry".

Four men set off from the Charpoua Hut with ropes and pitons, but found progress difficult with the snow and verglas. They only managed to reach Méhot at 17.30 hrs., just in time for another snow storm.

While all parties were busy trying to reach the summit in order to rescue the two Germans by descending towards them along the west ridge, a further party had started an attempt to reach them directly from the foot of the mountain. They had chosen the most difficult route, but also the most direct; due to its verticality it was also the least affected by snow. Gary Hemming was very familiar with the west face of the Dru. In 1962 he made the first ascent of the *American Direct* with his countryman, Royal Robbins.

On August 18th, Hemming had travelled to Courmayeur with his friend and climbing companion Lothar Mauch. The weather had improved on the Italian side of Mont Blanc, and conditions were perfect for two routes they had planned for some time. They had scraped up their last few coins to pay the toll for the Mont Blanc tunnel, but once in Courmayeur and reading the Dauphiné Libéré over a coffee, Hemming realised his error. "Lothar, what an idiot I am. I wanted to ask about those two Germans before leaving Chamonix." [2]

Lothar was not keen on the idea of changing plans. He grumbled about not having thought about this earlier, that they had just spent sixty francs to drive through the tunnel, and that it would be a waste of even more money just to turn back. He was a generous lad. Had he been in Chamonix, he would not have hesitated about joining the rescue. But now they were on the other side of the Alps, the weather was marvellous and there were so many fine routes waiting for them ... And anyway, the Germans were hardly alone; so many were already involved in the rescue.

"You're right Lothar, what can I say? I'll hitchhike if you don't want to go back. Or we could hitchhike together so we don't have to waste money on the tunnel. I have to go. I don't have a choice. I'm an experienced climber and that makes me responsible for difficult rescues. All climbers are responsible for mountain rescues, it's not just up to the guides and soldiers. And anyway, think about it! It'll be great, really big. Much better than the south face of the Aiguille Noire. The south face is only another summit to climb. This rescue is a great ascent - a real adventure. But what's most important is that it involves the lives of two persons, two companions. If we make it, it will mean a lot more than just another windy summit, don't you agree?" [3]

Lothar was won over and followed him.

Once back in Chamonix, Gary explained his idea to

---

[2] & [3] From the article by Gary Hemming in PARIS MATCH

the E.H.M. instructors. He would climb up the same route as the Germans and descend by the *American Direct*. "All the gear should still be in place. Fifteen vertical pitches, clean double ropes. A technical climb, clear-cut, no risk of avalanches or rock-falls."

The instructors' responses were far from friendly: what was he doing meddling in their business? "Everyone is already up there," they told him. "I'm still going up, give me a radio." They grumbled for a while, but eventually handed one over. Gary had got together a group of friends: Gilles Bodin and François Guillot, two young trainee guides from Chamonix; Mick Burke, an Englishman who had descended the *American Direct* the year before, with an injured companion in poor weather; and Gerhard Baur, a German Gary had met a few days before. With Gary and Lothar they made up a group of six. Their sacks filled with ropes, food and a good supply of water, they set off.

At 14.00 hrs. on Friday the 19th, they reached the top of the couloir, but it began to snow and they had to bivouac.

On Saturday morning they were still there when they heard voices from below. Someone else had had the same idea - René Desmaison and Vincent Mercié. Desmaison was the expert on the Mont Blanc massif. He knew the Dru by heart and had made the first winter ascent of the west face in 1957. He was an alpine guide, had taken part in numerous rescues and was furious because E.N.S.A., the official association for guides in Chamonix, was taking too much time deciding whether to join the rescue. Was this due to prudence, or rivalry with the E.H.M.? Desmaison, however, was not going to sit about waiting: Mercié was prepared to join him and they set off.

So now there were eight of them - too many for one party so they decided to separate into two groups: a lighter group who would try to reach the two ´shipwrecked´ - as they were now called - as soon as possible, and another to follow with gear and food.

"Apprehension on the west face of the Dru. The two German climbers shout to the Hemming-Desmaison team to hurry."

By this time, most of the rescue parties were nearing the ´shipwrecked´ Germans, still miraculously alive. Helicopter pilots from the Civil Defence and the police flew over the area whenever possible and came back with reassuring news: the two Germans were alive and still had the strength to get to their feet and reply to signals. Raymond Lambert, the Genevan pilot-guide, also carried out a daring flight in a Pilatus Porter owned by German television. By now the news had spread to the national newspapers and French television sent out live broadcasts on the rescue ...

On Friday there was a ´summit´ meeting with Jean Franco, director of E.N.S.A., Pierre Perret, president of the Chamonix guides and Lucien Dévies, president of the Fédération Française de la Montagne. Between them, they decided to send up a new party consisting of Yves Pollet-Villard and Yvon Masino from the Ecole Nationale d'Alpinisme, and two guides from Chamonix, Gérard Devouassoux and Christian Mollier. On Saturday, they were taken by helicopter to the foot of the north face. They had all agreed that the only way to reach the Germans was to ascend the easiest route and then traverse to the ledge.

At 15.30 hrs. Pollet-Villard radioed that they were making good progress and hoped to reach the exit of the Magnone route at the same time as Hemming and Desmaison (this was the first route on the west face, less direct than the *American*).

In the meantime, on the north-west ridge, Méhot and his group were recalled because their manoeuvres with the rope might have started rocks falling on the rescuers ascending the face directly. "Just when everything was starting to go so well!" protested Coudray, one of the trainee guides. He had already abseiled 120 metres and had fixed ropes for his companions. But orders were orders, and the Méhot party had to retreat.

Hemming and his group pegged their way up a 40-metre wall, one of the most difficult pitches which follows a crack where pitons and wooden wedges were still in place from previous ascents. One of the pitons came out under the weight of Desmaison.

"I'm off! Take in!" René's cry was heard by everyone - its significance made their blood run cold. Oh God please, no! Not another accident. Fortunately Vincent managed to stop René's fall. Bruised and grazed but with no serious injuries, René reached the ´jammed block´ with the others. This is a large boulder embedded in a small, rocky couloir. It was getting dark and the top of the boulder was a good place for a bivouac.

Helicopters flew in new rescue teams to strategic positions. The descent on the north face was being secured with ropes. The Dru was laid to siege.

"Rescued! Hemming and Desmaison reach the two Germans who have bivouacked for seven nights on the west face of the Dru."

At 06.00 hrs. Gary Hemming and François Guillot were moving quickly towards the pendulum traverse, the last obstacle between them and the two Germans. Finally, there they were! The two Germans were not injured and could move. René Desmaison had secured the corner for the descent but first he helped Gary and François with the two survivors to get back over the pendulum traverse. Once this tricky manoeuvre had been completed and reunited on a small ledge, the two Germans were plied with hot drinks and given dry clothes. Their names were Heinz Ramisch and Hermann Schriddel. They had only met recently in Chamonix, and had now gone through an ordeal together they would never forget. The other Germans at Montenvers also were strangers until a few days ago, but they had all rushed together to rescue these two. (Unknown to the group reunited on the terrace, a friend of the Germans, Wolfgang Egle, was at the time descending the north face on a double rope. There was a lot of snow and ice, Wolfgang was tired, maybe he made a mistake on a manoeuvre; he got entwined in his rope and was strangled.)

Hemming's group was preoccupied with getting Ramisch and Schriddel down. Pollet-Villard had reached the corner on the north face. He had received instructions from the ´Joint Chiefs of Staff´ in the valley: "You have to get the two Germans down the north face." René Desmaison did not even spare a thought to these instructions. The two survivors were exhausted and they would never be able to do the traverse in their condition. It would also take too much time to help them traverse the other face with a series of rope-pulley manoeuvres, and they could not risk getting caught in another storm. The best solution would be to lower them down the route they had used for the ascent. Hemming agreed with René and they began the complicated but secure series of manoeuvres. At 16.00 hrs. they reached a small terrace which could accommodate all ten and decided to bivouac there. Another stormy night was spent on the mountain. Bolts of lightning ferociously assaulted the Dru, spreading electric discharges over the rocks which lashed painfully at the climbers huddled against the rock face. Fortunately they were tied on to pitons and no-one was hurled off their terrace. It started to snow. They were all ready to leave just before dawn broke. Luckily the weather improved and they could continue with their manoeuvres, slowly but steadily. As it began to get dark they arrived at the base of the face, on the Dru glacier.

Yet another bivouac was necessary, but this time in comfortable tents, curled up in dry, down sleeping bags.

CHAPTER TWO

A Hero is Born

The public, who had followed the rescue operation for so many days, now wanted to get a closer look at the people involved. A crowd awaited them on the Dru glacier, and even more people had gathered in Chamonix where they arrived the next day, flown in by helicopter. Celebrations rang round the village, for the success of the rescue, the survivors, the rescuers, but most of all, people wanted to celebrate the hero of the moment, Gary Hemming.

The papers were full of him, he was the only one to appear on television; it almost seemed that he had carried out the rescue single handed, almost as if there had never been such a considerable deployment of the forces of E.H.M., E.N.S.A. and the Civil Defence. Even Hemming's companions were neglected, including René Desmaison who also did everything in his power during the rescue, and who shared with Gary the winning idea of climbing directly up to the Germans. The local papers set aside only a few lines for the scandalous news of his expulsion from the Association of Guides on grounds of insubordination -

the petty revenge of authority for its loss of face. Desmaison was a famous climber, he played a decisive part in this rescue and the injustice he had to suffer was manifest. But all eyes were on the American: everyone wanted a picture of him; everyone wanted to interview him. Everyone was talking about Gary.

A journalist from Paris Match was at Chamonix to report on the rescue, and was without doubt influenced by the previous day´s news which had focused on the actions of Gary Hemming. When he met Gary, he was struck by his appearance: "If there is one thing you notice when you meet him for this first time, it's not his height: it's his figure - a thin build, almost bony, all angles, and his formidable strawberry blonde hair, like a doll's, quite simply sticks up from his head and falls down impartially on all sides... Under the shadow of his fringe are two cheeky, bright eyes between which his pointed nose accentuates his vaguely unearthly look. Red jumper, patched breeches, makeshift clothes...." [4]. He had appeared every summer for years in Chamonix like this. He was a familiar figure but up to that point, apart from the climbers who respected him for his new ascents on Mont Blanc, no-one had really thought of him other than as a picturesque ragamuffin.

Pierre Joffroy, the journalist from Paris Match, was struck not only by Gary's appearance. Something about the American impressed him. Joffroy had an idea: get Gary to write the feature article. At first Gary refused. He said that he was not a good writer, but in truth he was exhausted. Joffroy was patient and implacable. He travelled with him back to the Hotel de Paris and did not leave his side until

[4] From an article written by Pierre Joffroy in PARIS MATCH, "Dans la tourmente du Dru, un héros est né".

Gary had completed the article. When it was published it was a great success. It was written in the staccato style of the 60s, and was striking in its vital images and for the novelty of its content. There had never been such an article written about a climbing event, with very few technical details - normally incomprehensible for the majority of readers - but one in which a human story emerged, including references to what was happening in the world around - the Vietnam war, the earthquake in Turkey ...

Pierre Joffroy was very enthusiastic about his discovery. As a writer, a friend of artists and an artist himself, Joffroy had helped several young people to cultivate their talents. And now he enthusiastically supported the new talent discovered in Gary: he was to encourage and assist him throughout the years to come and would play an important role after Gary's death.

During the next few days in Chamonix, and later when he returned to Paris, Gary experienced the giddy heights of fame. His face was on the covers of numerous magazines and on television; everyone recognised him, stopped him in the street, greeted him, asked him for an autograph. Taxi drivers would stop to say hello to him, young boys would follow him, hanging on to his jumper; he received dozens of letters from women who claimed to have fallen head over heels in love with him.

At first he was amused by it all, and naturally flattered. But deep down, just as with his favourite Jack London character, Martin Eden, he could not escape from the bitter, sardonic aspect to his moment of glory. "I am still the same person I was before. Before I was already me, just as I am now. Why then did no-one notice me? Why was I shunned, pitied?"

Who knew what Marie would think? Who knew what his parents would think? They would read the papers, watch the television.

Marie was the lost love of Gary's life. He had first met her in Chamonix in 1962. They separated after a few months, and since then they had got back together and split numerous times. But some time ago, Marie had put her trust in the protective environment of her family and no longer wanted to see him. Gary was born a knight-errant, the champion of the weak. By a striking coincidence, his real name was Gareth, like the knight of King Arthur, prince of the Orkneys who suffered such a sad fate. Gary the champion could not live without ideals and without an ideal love. And just then, his ideal love Marie refused to see him, even to talk to him. What wouldn't he do to earn requited love, to attract her attention - solo ascents, journeys to all ends of the world each time she deigned to see him. He had written her hundreds of pages, dedicated every worthy action to her.

And now, without planning, he had performed the most marvellous, noble deed, and everyone had recognised him for it. Maybe now Marie would be moved into seeing him.

As soon as he returned to Paris, Gary went to Fonteney where she lived. He had not managed to telephone. He had written a letter but received no reply. But if Marie were to see him in person, then surely she would not refuse to speak to him ... No she could not refuse

... But Marie did. Gary was determined to speak to her, just talk, explain ... Marie could not avoid an explanation, had to talk to him. "Some day soon even the Americans will have to talk to the Vietcong: Marie must talk with me." He knew that she was in the house and did not hesitate: he climbed over the hedge and her parents called the police.

He got off with a scolding: after all his face was famous even in the police station, and how could you put a national hero in jail? OK it was illegal entry, but for such a romantic cause ... And anyway, word was sent to Pierre Mazeaud (a renowned Alpinist, Himalayan mountaineer, writer and an influential politician), who vouched for him.

During his period of glory, Gary was also given the opportunity to establish himself as a writer. He had always had a passion for writing, and had a pair of projects which were very dear to him. One was a study of climbing in California, and the other an autobiography with the curious title *Patchwork of Research*, which tells of his experiences as a climber and as a man. It was half finished, in English. A Parisian publisher who was keen on the idea of publishing the work of the hero of the moment, entered into a contract with Gary, paid him a sum in advance, rented an apartment for him and arranged for a typewriter and translator. Gary applied himself to the completion of his autobiography with the fervent zeal he applied to everything he believed in, and the manuscript was soon finished. But unfortunately the publisher, who was expecting a mountaineering book, found himself presented with an extravagant accumulation of passages interrupted by letters and their envelopes, notes, sketches, aeroplane

and bus tickets, poems, written on a slant, back to front ...
Gary was convinced of the value of his work. It represented
his own thoughts, his story. Those were the episodes of his
life, his being. Even the envelopes, even the old scraps -
nothing according to Gary should be thrown away: "I am
my own rubbish bin", he melodramatically declared.

Gary had not had a permanent home since he left
the States in 1960. He lived with friends here and there, his
only address was poste restante. He liked to send postcards
of the Seine on which he would mark, under a bridge, "this
is where I live". But in his friends' houses, papers written
by Gary were piling up. These were his diaries, the letters
he received, copies of the letters he wrote, documents,
certificates, newspaper clippings; drafts of letters, sketches,
projects and dreams. He had either carried everything with
him when he travelled, or left his papers with a friend, but
keeping a strict inventory of everything. And ´Patchwork of
Research´ was nothing more than an accumulation of all
these papers, the sum of his whole life. The publisher,
however, was very confused. He eventually decided not
to publish the book ´due to technical problems´.

Despite its failure, this had been an opportunity
which would never have been open to Gary had it not been
for the fame he achieved from the rescue on the Dru.

Fame is like a strong spirit. Whilst taking great gulps of it,
you eventually forget its bitter aftertaste. When its effect
wears off, you can suffer from serious withdrawal
symptoms. Many of Gary's friends believe that fame went
to Gary's head. Not that he became conceited - he was
sincere in his mockery of those who admired him, but

became furious if not recognised immediately or if an acknowledgement was not sincere. He had finally got used to being pointed out and celebrated, and besides, it was a part of his contradictory nature to want to be the centre of attention with those around him. It was a sad time for him when he felt himself disappearing back into the mist of anonymity.

Pierre Mazeaud is convinced that Gary's fame was the main cause of his death. "Gary was a profound, sensitive, passionate man. He suffered a great deal from the false fame achieved after the rescue on the Dru and the extensive newspaper coverage of the event. He suffered first from his popularity which interfered with his private life, and later from the abandonment and ridicule. When Gary went back to the States, his friends were amused by his new status: 'Here he is, the hero!' Maybe subsequent delusion was not the only cause of his death, but I believe that it helped quicken it."

Mazeaud, a lawyer and a deeply cultured man, had been a Government Minister and a State Councillor on several occasions. A climber himself, he was close to Gary for several years and Gary often lived in his houses, in Chamonix and in the rue de la Victoire, Paris. Pierre Mazeaud found Gary fascinating: "He enriched my life. He enriched the perceptions I have of humankind. He has given new meaning to experiences. If I had never met him, I would not have today the same philosophical perception of people and things".

Pierre Mazeaud paced up and down his elegant study in the Marais quarter, staring ahead as he spoke. He chose his words with care: it was obvious that he was used to talking in public. But behind the impersonality of the skilled orator lay a fervent emotion which still burned.

It was the same emotion which still links Gary's friends, twenty years on, when remembering him. Such strength of emotion, after such a long time, is striking. What kind of man was he, who was able to imprint himself so deeply on the souls of those who knew him?

CHAPTER THREE

An Extraordinary Liar

During the months after the rescue on the Dru, Gary stayed in Paris. He lived between Mazeaud and Joffroy until he moved into the small apartment rented for him by his publisher. He lived frugally, as always, on the small sum of money he received monthly from America; a pension for veterans of the Korean war, or so he said, awarded despite him never having set foot in Korea. On other occasions, he said that his mother sent these monthly payments.

When it came to his private life, Gary was extraordinarily secretive and even refused to reveal his age. "Today I am fifty years old. Yesterday, however, I was twenty five," he would reply on being questioned about his age. As a rule, he would claim he was younger than he actually was, but pretence of youth was not the purpose for his reticence. Rather it was irritation at others having personal information about him, as if this knowledge would allow strangers access to something that was his only - a part of his soul. It was for this reason that he never talked about his childhood, or when he did, in only the vaguest terms. One month after the rescue, during an interview carried out for Elle magazine, Gary replied without inhibitions on the question of drugs, and in fact launched into a eulogy on LSD. When questioned about his age, however, he once again refused to answer: "I don't have an age. I refuse to answer that question." He was also very elusive about his family: "My father was a gangster and my mother was a saint." [5] He had told some of his friends that his father was in prison, at Sing Sing, but to others, the prison was Alcatraz.

It is possible that his father had got into trouble with the law, because his mother divorced him just before Gary started school. She was a very conventional woman, and if her husband was in prison, she would not have put up with Gary being called the son of a convict by his school friends. However, the reason behind the divorce could be more simple. Maybe her husband had left her, or she had left him. But one thing remains - the absence of his father during Gary's childhood, and maybe the hurt he felt from not having a father, had led him to picture his mother as an innocent victim and a saint, while his father was guilty and a criminal.

Gary was fond of theatrical exaggeration, and of making a fool of everyone.

"Once I was one metre sixty high. But during the war the Japanese pulled me by the head and feet. Now I am one metre ninety," he would tell the television, with a straight face, only to add directly afterwards: "None of that is true. The real truth is that I was born one metre ninety." [6]

[5] From article in ELLE no. 1086 of 13.10.66.

[6] From article in PARIS MATCH

Jerry Gallwas, his childhood friend and first climbing companion, says that:" He was an extraordinary liar. I've never known anyone like him. He could look you right in the eyes, with a straight face and tell you the most incredible lies. And then he would roll around laughing because you fell for it."

In one of Pierre Joffroy's novels, there is a character named Sholto who resembles Gary - tall, lanky, with long, blonde hair, patched trousers, red jumper and a scarf trailing on the ground. This character moves with a discordantly light step among the tragic characters of a painful existence, solving dramatic events by means of farcical schemes.

This is the image Gary left behind, the image imprinted on the minds of those who met him. A vital character who does not fit into this world, both hero and clown at the same time. The reconstruction of his life based on testimony is an extremely difficult task, as those who knew him remember only this image of an elf, of profane joker and not those small, concrete facts which would allow the writer to reconstruct events and pigeonhole these in a chronological order.

Gary for his part, did all he could to cover his footsteps, moving as quick as the wind from one country to another, and then going back to the same countries, the same women, in such a giddy whirl of events that you lose all sense of dates.

Leave no trace. This was a principle for Gary, almost an obsession. Lothar Mauch remembers a large number of routes he climbed with Gary which Gary would not let him talk about. "We climbed many difficult routes -

sometimes first ascents - and when we got back to the hut, people would ask; ´What did you do?´ because they probably had seen us climbing. Gary , on every occasion, would reply; ´Only a short stroll´. He really could not stand those people who could not wait to boast about their climbs."

Jerry Gallwas can also remember climbs with Gary in California, at Tahquitz Rock and Joshua Tree, which they did not record, and told no-one about. They had become skilled climbers and had begun to open new routes, but Gary did not want to leave any traces on the rock - they took everything away with them, pitons and slings - and he never wanted to talk to others about these routes.

However all this secrecy is sharply contradicted by the routes achieved during 1962 and '63 on Mont Blanc with Robbins, Harlin and Frost: routes which received considerable media coverage to which Gary was not totally opposed.

Gary´s life was an ongoing contradiction. The desire to pass lightly through existence without leaving traces was in direct contrast with his continual need for approval and admiration, which led him to perform flamboyant acts. He liked to scandalise people with his untidy appearance and frequent use of profanities, but it hurt him when people judged him by his appearance. He was a fervent pacifist, but would often turn to violence and was capable of physically attacking anyone who made him lose his temper. He claimed to be a tolerant person, but was arrogant and domineering when it came to defending his principles. "I will not tolerate any form of intolerance except intolerance of intolerance," [7] he would candidly declare.

[7] From his diaries

28

Although sensitive and generous, he could make use of malicious tricks to get what he wanted. He took what he wanted and what he could get without scruples; but he followed a very strict moral code to which he frequently referred. He seemed to have a pressing need to assert his personality: he was prepared to act dishonestly in order to achieve that which he considered his by right. But at other times he would suffer abject humiliation in order to receive forgiveness or acceptance. He was brave to the extent of recklessness, but was petrified of ´getting caught in a trap´ and would flee from all responsibility. At other times, however, he would take on disproportionate obligations.

Every man is made up of contradictions, but those contained within Gary were substantial and formed a way of life. How does one manage to get through each day, with two different minds constantly fighting each other?

The French gave him the nickname of ´the Beatnik of the Alps´. He was opposed to this name. "I am not a beatnik. This is a pejorative term for parasites with long hair. They are characterised as refusing life... At first, in San Francisco, the beatnik movement was something else. It was based on Zen Buddhism and spiritual discipline. In the west we are able to follow an exterior and formal school. Without it there would be no roads, offices, aeroplanes. But we have forgotten about the inner and spiritual dimensions. In fact, it is almost impossible to exist as an authentic beatnik. You have to live at a compromise with society." [8]

Maybe the name ´hippie´ would have been better suited, but Gary would not accept any form of labelling, and refused to admit that he belonged to any form of

[8] From article in ELLE no. 1086 of 13.10.66.

movement or group. He claimed total originality with regard to his appearance and behaviour.

Gary expected a recognition which he constantly craved, and when this was lacking, he suffered painful identity crises, drowning himself in contradictions. He wrote in his diary:

"My name is Gary. Gary Hemming. My name is George. George Schlief. My name is Jean. Jean Paul Sartre. My name is Walter. Walter Fuckall. My name is Walter. Walter Bonatti. My name is John. John Anybody. My name is Charles. Charles de Gaulle. And yours? What is your name, tell it please. We are all eager to know. To know your identity. Do you have an identity? Or have you lost it somewhere! Or did you ever have one? My identity is Gary, and yours? What do you do? Everyone knows Gary. Alpinist at large. He's done all the big ones, you know. In the Alps. He's made the reputation of American climbers in Europe something. Really something. Gary's a big climber. He's an important man. He's been around. Ask him what he's climbed. You won't believe it.

"Can you believe it? Now I know with certainty the impossible situation of being ´somebody important´ and you know that everybody knows you're somebody important. You strut. You find a spare window to admire your tousled hair and your boyish grin, your artful way of talking. You're magnificent, aren't you. You're somebody. And anybody that's somebody acts magnificently. Isn't that true?

"How would you like to have to walk into every room everywhere for all your life in the same manner you did this eve at the American Alpine Club meeting? A little call at the Delmontes in the Calendale hills looking out over half of Los Angeles County. Everyone else wore coats and ties. But you - you knew better - what's this coat and tie shit? - Levis and sandals in what I went every day now - that's what I'll wear tonite. And they'll accept it. They won't say anything. Shit. They wouldn't dare. You're somebody. You're Gary Hemming the big alpinist. Fuck all your cunts. I'll wear what I please. I'm a wheel.

"How would you like to be able to walk about in an atmosphere such as that one all your life?

"Fuck Fuck Fuck.

"This is what Sartre was trying to say when he refused the Nobel Prize. This is where he showed himself a big hypocrite. He already is an institution, Nobel Prize or no. But certainly one when he's the only one to ever refuse this Prize! Shit. He's doomed. He's an institution. His name is. His face is. Everything about him is. You're a doomed man, Jean Paul. I feel sorry for you. No artist can hold up to this. An artist is the common man thinking, living and recording in the fashion easiest and most satisfying for him to record. NO more NO less. The artist is not an institution. This artist is not a name. He's not important.

"He's not even an IDENTITY to others. He's their identity of themselves perhaps. But he's never his identity of himself. He's ZERO. Everybody is an artist. If you want to be an artist just go and record." [9]

---

[9] From his diaries

CHAPTER FOUR

The Salad Days

Gary was born in Pasadena, Los Angeles county, on December 13th 1934. His mother, Carmen, was young - only 19-years old when she had Gary but Carmen was his father's second wife. They lived in Columbus, Ohio, but Carmen travelled often to visit her parents in Los Angeles, and Gary was born during one of these visits.

Carmen was very attached to her mother and family. They were a large, happy family. All the girls loved to go out dancing and never missed a party, to which they were always escorted by their brothers, or some uncle - they were all brought up under strict religious principles and a sacred respect of manners. Gary would recount that his grandmother had washed his mouth out with soap and a brush because he swore. The result of this punishment was apparently not so effective as, for the rest of his life, Gary seemed to derive great pleasure from adorning his conversations with picturesque obscenities.

Gary's mother often told Gary stories of her family and her favourite uncle. Uncle Danny was Carmen's mother's half-brother and a captain in the navy. When Carmen´s family moved to California, he had already been transferred to onshore work, in harbour master's offices in various towns. But in his youth, he had sailed many seas, and had become a friend of Jack London. Apparently, after Dan was put to shore work, London would seek him out every time he turned up in the towns where Dan was working (he had been transferred from Oregon to Washington State and then to California). Together they would disappear for days on end. Eventually they would reappear with tales of colossal drunken nights which Dan would recall for weeks afterwards.

Carmen was very beautiful: tall, blonde, with a cheeky nose and the mischievous eyes of her son. Gary's father was also described as a handsome man - tall, with an impressive voice and hair the colour of flame. He was an engineer and had worked in a small family business until his father threw him out because of some mistake. No-one knows what this mistake was, but it must have been serious, for his parents to reject him. Gary once recounted a visit he made to them - without his mother knowing - and his grandparents refused to recognise him as their grandchild.

Robert Hemming had a passion for gambling. He was particularly fond of poker, but was also known to speculate on the markets. It is quite probable that this pastime was the reason behind his encounter with the law, if he ever did have such problems. The puritanical Carmen could certainly never have accepted his gambling and did everything in her power to prevent her son being influenced by her husband - she even went so far as never to speak to him of his father. Another of Robert's characteristics which Carmen feared was his arrogance. Gary could vaguely remember a time when he was a young child and was in the car with his parents. His father was driving very fast, speeding round bends, and Carmen, scared to death, asked him to slow down. Every time she asked him to slow down, he would accelerate, obviously enjoying her fear. He remembered that this episode ended with Carmen getting out of the car with Gary in her arms and walking back.

Carmen loved her husband and their separation must have hurt a great deal. She must have also suffered from the efforts she made to wipe him out of her memory, in an attempt to protect Gary. Despite these efforts, however, she could not prevent the love of risk and an element of violence being passed on to her son.

Gary grew up in a female environment with his mother, his grandmother and a young aunt, only six years older than him. He thought of his aunt as an older sister and they were very close. One year before Gary started at school, Carmen divorced her husband, settled down in San Diego and got a job.

Gary worked hard at school and was an obedient and respectful son: Carmen had nothing to complain of. He could be stubborn at times, and would keep to his principles although they conflicted with those of his mother. Also he began early on to theorise and discuss general subjects, a habit he never lost. Carmen, however, was more pragmatic and tended to reduce all conversation to small, concrete, day-to-day facts. Not able to find a suitable conversation partner for his favourite discussions, Gary began to entrust his philosophical speculations to pen and paper.

When he was fourteen years old, he moved up to the High School at La Mesa. This was a period of growth for him: his first friendships, his first love, trips to the Sierra and, on his first climb, the striking realisation of his passion for climbing, and the decision that he would become a great climber, in addition to being a famous author.

In the meantime, Carmen had remarried and this probably came as a relief to Gary: he felt more free now that Carmen had a husband to care for and worry about. Gary's relationship with his stepfather was good: an adult relationship, not particularly affectionate but built on mutual respect.

Having received a high school diploma in mathematics and science, Gary enrolled at the San Diego State University in 1952. He attended classes there, on and off, for a couple of years, was impatient to learn everything - he enrolled in courses for geometry, chemistry, geology, astronomy, economics, philosophy, psychology, Russian and Spanish - and at the same time he trained rigorously to improve the level of his climbing achievements. Winter weekends were spent in the Sierra, travelling great distances on skis, and every free moment he had during the summer he climbed in the Californian mountains. Every so often, he would give up his favourite sport in order to earn money from some desultory job. His first full-time job was during the summer of 1954, at Jackson Hole in Wyoming, as a worker in a tractor repair shop.

In 1955 military service took him off to the state of New York, and later on to Kentucky for a parachute training course. Gary had to make a great effort to accept military discipline, with all its unreasonable limitations. But Gary was brought up during a period of cult patriotism, and besides he had decided to use this transitory period to learn new sporting disciplines and to study. For ´veterans´, after one year of military service, there was the opportunity to enrol in a preliminary course which would eventually lead to a Masters Degree - Gary threw himself into this course with great zeal.

Eventually, Gary realised the advantages of his situation. To be able to study free of charge in the United States was valuable, and once he had completed his conscription, Gary considered prolonging his military service. He wanted to enrol at West Point Academy, but his stepfather, who wrote frequently to Gary during his military service, encouraged him to enrol in the Air Force Academy at Colorado Springs instead. This academy was one of the most prestigious and most highly disciplined military schools in the whole of the USA, founded with the purpose of forming a corps of ´hard´ officers, adapted to the changing needs of the new America. The Korean war was hardly over and the threat of the Vietnam war was appearing on the horizon. Those were the years of heroic films which portrayed the American soldier as the defender of western civilisation.

The Air Force Academy was a factory for superhumans, each one capable, at the end of their training, of carrying out missions alone which, during the Second World War, would have required the intervention of a squadron of bomber pilots. An officer, having gone through the Academy, had to be able to carry out any mission assigned to him, irrespective of location or circumstances and without being able to count on the help or support of anyone; and he had to have a high share of character, courage and patriotism. He had to be of athletic build, which would allow him to perform amazing tasks, have nerves of steel, a quick mind, be capable of absorbing knowledge of sophisticated techniques, have the courage to survive in enemy territory, be capable of taking command, and have the certainty to be able to face any emergency.

The training necessary to create such a superhuman was extremely hard, and at its core, naturally, lay the iron hand of discipline, deliberately repressive. Primarily, the trainee officer had to be cleansed of his personality so that he could be transformed into the perfect military robot the Academy had promised to provide for the USA. Every second during a day was regulated, even outside of training hours: how you were to walk, how you addressed your superiors and your companions, how to sit down in the lecture room and at dinner table.

Gary only remained at the Academy for four months. During his time in Europe, he said that he was thrown out for lack of discipline, and made jokes about the absurd regulations in the Academy; but strangely enough, among his papers, which he kept and ordered so carefully, and in his diaries, there is no mention of this event. There are only a few vague references, written at times when he was at a low ebb, to 'that tragic evening' and to the subsequent

´dishonour´. However, among his papers is the ´honourable discharge´ dated 17th December 1956, testimonial from the Academy of a ´faithful and honest service´.

What could have driven Gary to invent such a serious event as expulsion from the Academy? Maybe the atmosphere in 1960s France had amplified his concept of freedom, and the image of rebel which he had created and in which he strongly believed, led him to disapprove of his youthful choice of career. He was going through a process of achieving ideological maturity and was very critical of the political choices being made in his country. Expulsion on the grounds of lack of discipline from a very exclusive military academy, where it had been a merit to be accepted, really was completely in character for the new Gary.

On the other hand, there are hints in his diary of other circumstances, and besides, expulsion after four months from such an academy is hardly a straightforward affair. If the expulsion had been on grounds of health or any other reason, Gary would have talked about this and written it down.

His friends often asked themselves if Gary was telling the truth. Maybe the person nearest to the truth is Claude. She was the person closest to Gary, even when he was light years away from her:

"The Air Force Academy was without doubt an important period for Gary. Firstly because he wanted to learn to fly. Don't forget that flying is one of the first ambitions for an adventurous youth, who loves freedom. And to be accepted by the Academy was a great honour, a coveted goal. Gary was accepted because he passed all the fitness tests, and this must have really pleased him, but then he found himself caught up in an endless series of obligations and regulations which he neither understood nor approved of - he couldn't help rebelling against them.

"When he talked about his expulsion, he said that it was due to the fact that people were unfair. He never wanted to go further with this discussion, but I think that what happened was that while everyone cheated secretly, he wanted to flout the rules openly. Because of this, his punishment was severe as an example to discourage others.

"Maybe later, realising that the punishment was excessive, the authorities amended his discharge paper to 'honourable discharge' so as not to subject Gary to ferocious defamatory condemnation - in the United States you have to present your certificate of discharge on numerous occasions: to enrol at university, when looking for a job. This punishment would have been too much for someone who had only been incautious enough to do openly what others had always done in secret."

CHAPTER FIVE

No Half Dome for Gary

Military service intervened in Gary's most coveted dream: the first ascent of the NW face of the Half Dome in Yosemite Valley.

He discovered his passion for the mountains during his years at the High School in La Mesa and in particular during a trip to Baja California. This trip made a great impression on him. Maurice Camillo invited him on this Sierra Club outing and Gary, for the first time, had the opportunity to spend several days in a deserted landscape, sleeping out in the open without the shelter of a tent, and climbing on apparently virgin rock faces. This experience proved unforgettable for Gary, remaining a constant point of reference in his future ascents.

Among the group of climbers in the Sierra Club was Dick Long, with whom Gary struck up a friendship. He visited Dick often, hitchhiking to San Francisco Bay to go climbing or skiing with him in Northern California - cross-country skiing naturally, as downhill skiing was still in its initial stages in California. Gary and Dick used piste skis with army surplus sealskins. During these trips Gary discovered a convenient system for spending the cold winter nights without it costing a dime. In California there was a custom that in the village prisons - and in the west even the tiniest village had its own prison - the homeless can get a roof over their heads, on the condition that they leave at dawn the next day. Gary took advantage of this hospitality - to the point that, if he had not first travelled to San Francisco, he would arrange to meet Dick at 06.00 hrs., at the prison gates of some village situated at the foot of the mountains.

During those years, Gary was also friendly with Jerry Gallwas and George Schlief, avid climbers themselves. Jerry turned out to be one of the key figures during the great period of classic first ascents in Yosemite. The trio's first ascents took place in the area round La Mesa. Later on, George managed to get hold of an old car with which they could move around more freely.

California has a vast landscape, scattered with deep valleys and superb mountains. However, the distances between these are great. From San Diego it takes several hours to drive to the Mojave desert with its expanse of granite blocks, such as Joshua Tree. Closer to the city is Tahquitz Rock, the favourite area for Gary and his friends. After having climbed all the most famous routes there, they embarked on new routes of ever-increasing difficulty, in search of an impossible perfection.

To reach Yosemite Valley took a full day for Gary, but once he had tasted its marvels, he went back as often as he could. The valley constitutes only a small part of Yosemite National Park which stretches over almost three thousand square kilometres to the east of San Francisco. It is an enchanted valley of towering granite ramparts from which cascade crystal waterfalls. Along its bed the Merced River runs, banked by forests of sequoia and mariposa pine which are suddenly cut off by the precipitous rock walls soaring up over several thousand feet.

The valley was discovered by chance in 1851 by a group of soldiers hunting down Indians who had pillaged an encampment of pioneers. The valley soon became a popular area for tourist and walkers. However, rock-climbing was a late arrival, if we overlook the ascents of the main peaks. Mountaineers arrived in the 40s and 50s, with their sophisticated techniques and, latterly, chrome-molybdenum pitons, which allowed them to master the smooth, vertical walls of compact granite.

Half Dome is situated at the end of the valley and is easily recognised by its distinctive outline of a large dome cut neatly in half, as if by a gigantic axe. In 1865, there was an article in the California Geological Survey which described the peak as: 'A crest of granite... perfectly inaccessible, being probably the only one of all the prominent points about Yosemite which never has been, and never will be, trodden by human foot.' However, only ten years later, the Scot George Anderson, a carpenter and road builder, managed to surmount its eastern wall using iron pegs to drill the rock, and ropes. The curved flank of the dome was now accessible. However, from that date, almost 100 years passed before the north-west face - the six hundred metres of vertical rock cropped by the imaginary axe - was ascended.

On Gary's first visit to Yosemite, he was captivated by the impressive structure of Half Dome and his imagination began to take over. He had never made an ascent of anything similar to that smooth wall of perfectly vertical rock, precariously overhanging in some points. It was like a mirror. What could be more magic than climbing a mirror? It was an irresistible challenge.

Gary did climb some routes in the valley with Dick; they opened a few new routes of average difficulty, but also ascended the most difficult route in the valley: the *Steck-Salathè* on Sentinel Rock - the 1950 forerunner of the age of routes on vast rock faces. Then with Jerry Gallwas, he climbed some of the most demanding routes in the valley. Jerry was good company and a talented climber, but Half Dome was then considered too big an undertaking for a rope of two. They would have to organise a proper attempt, studied thoroughly in advance. It would require at least two parties with extra ropes to pull up the necessary materials and supplies for the amount of time they would spend on the face.

Meanwhile Gary got to know other climbers in the valley. He enjoyed climbing with two in particular, Wally Kodis and Wayne Merry, and invited them onto the project. However, Wayne was conscripted and transferred to Hawaii, where he kept fit by climbing on the volcanoes: they corresponded regularly and continually improved the plan of attack on the north-west face of Half Dome. They studied in detail the gear they intended to use and having heard talk of Dacron ropes, said to be more durable and less elastic than nylon ropes and as such more suited as fixed ropes, they intended to use it to secure the face with rope as they proceeded so that the second party could climb up and haul supplies. They searched for a drill with a carbon bit to help them pierce the compact granite for those areas where there were no piton cracks and where they needed extra protection. Bivouacking would be another problem due to the lack of ledges large enough to sit on. The Schmid brothers, during their first ascent of the north face of the Matterhorn, had used a bivouac hammock hung on pitons: Gary and Wayne considered copying this idea, but using cloth hammocks which would be lighter to carry. They discussed the number and type of pitons, the length of rope, how the two parties should proceed - one after the other, or alternating.

During this time, Gary also had to leave on military service, but his absence did not prevent him from nursing his ambition and keeping his friends interested. It was Wally's resolve that started to weaken.

Jerry, however, continued to visit Yosemite and got to know the best climbers there - Royal Robbins, Warren Harding, Chuck Pratt, Don Wilson. In June 1955, Jerry Gallwas, along with Robbins, Harding and Wilson, made an attempt on the north-west face of Half Dome. They had to retreat after some 150 metres, but when Gary heard of this attempt, several months afterwards, he was furious - they were trying to steal his glory!

He increased his correspondence with Wayne and Wally: "We have to beat Jerry & Co. to the Half Dome!" Gary's aggressiveness put Wally off for good: "I think that this 'succeed or die' attitude can only have an ill-omened effect on any party attempting Half Dome."

In the summer of 1956 Gary was busy with the admission examination for the Air Force Academy. When he left the Academy, he moved to Oakland in San Francisco Bay. He was determined to continue the studies started during his military service and enrolled in the university, in the engineering faculty, and took on door to door selling of encyclopaedias to make a living. In Oakland he was closer to Yosemite and travelled there often. During this time, he met new friends and changed his climbing companions. He also turned more and more to solo climbing, and was increasingly drawn by the appeal of distant mountains. He wanted to climb all the mountains in the world! For now he made do with the mountains in the west and went back to the Tetons, with which he had been fascinated ever since his first time there with Mort Hempel, when he spent the summer working at Jackson Hole.

During the summer, he bumped into John Harlin, whom he had met in 1954 in Yosemite when they had taken part in a rescue together. John's personality was the antithesis of Gary's, but they shared a passion for the mountains, for open space, for adventure, and their opposite natures were strangely attracted. Soon they started to climb together. John had already climbed the great northern peaks, had already been in the Alps, and Gary made use of John's experience during an ascent of Mount Rainier to learn ice techniques, of which he was completely ignorant. In July, they joined Henry Kendall and Hobey DeStaebler on a short trip to the Battle Range group in British Columbia, Canada. This mountainous area, a part of the Selkirk Range, stretches thirty kilometres as the crow flies to the south of the Glacier Circle, but is separated from the Glacier Circle by three mountain ranges and two vast glaciers. Access to this area from the north had still not been discovered, and the existing maps were filled with extensive blanks. This presented the type of adventure Gary had always dreamed of - a region of forests, foaming rivers, glaciers and snow-covered mountains on which Gary and his companions were the first men to tread. They would find a crossing and climb some peaks. Preparations for this trip took up all of Gary's time and he forgot his obsession with Half Dome.

The expedition to British Columbia was the closest thing to Gary's real concept of the mountain. Later on, when he rejected the label of mountaineer and announced that he was ´an adventurer´, he had discovered what he was always searching for in the mountains: much more than the struggle to overcome difficult routes and the glory of a first ascent, he aspired to open spaces where he was free to use his imagination and to travel - ´the frontier´.

The summer of 1957 came to an end. In June of that year, Jerry Gallwas climbed the north-west face of Half Dome with Royal Robbins and Mike Sherrick. The main character in this ascent was Robbins, who went on to make some of the hardest ascents of the ´big walls´ in Yosemite, with minimal use of artificial aid. Other famous routes from the golden years in Yosemite were opened up by Warren Harding, who exploited the use of artificial aids. These two great mountaineers had adopted different ethical approaches to artificial climbing and each defended their own positions with pride, turning their backs on each other with disdain.

In 1958 Wayne Merry climbed El Capitan with Harding by way of the first great route, *The Nose*. He did not take part in the ascent of the Half Dome, but helped with three friends transport supplies by rope, ascending the normal route, secured with iron pegs on the east side. He left notes at a ´viewpoint´ for other climbers ascending the normal route, warning that there were climbers on the face below them: ´Please do not throw down stones´.

When Gary heard of the ascent of Half Dome, he was content. By now his imagination was occupied with other ascents, in different locations.

CHAPTER SIX

On the Banks of Jenny Lake

1958 was nearing its end and the opportunity for an unusual job interrupted Gary's engineering studies at the University of California. The State of California Water Department offered him 25 dollars per day - a good salary in those days - as a ´Snow Surveyor´ in the Sierra Nevada. This involved checking the depth of snow in different areas of the Sierra, in order to be able to forecast the volumes of water in the melts which feed the reservoirs for the cities on the Pacific coast. A team of two would ski through mountainous snow-covered regions, taking surveys at points on their journey. The wooden cabins where they spent the night were some distance apart, and the trips demanded at least eight hours on skis per day, and this for a strong skier. This was the perfect job for Gary who loved, more than anything, to work out of doors. Unfortunately, the subsequent winter, the State of California started using helicopters in order to transport surveyors for this work, and they no longer needed talented alpinists.

The following summer, Gary longed for open spaces and snow-covered mountains. After a winter working on the Sierra, Yosemite Valley with its crowds and oppressive heat seemed jaded. He wanted to climb unknown mountains in deserted regions, as the year before in British Columbia. He managed to convince two friends, Sterling Neale and Dave Dornan whom he had met the previous summer in the Tetons, to join him on a trip to the Cariboo Range in British Columbia, where they climbed several unnamed peaks.

On returning from Canada, Gary was broke, but it was the start of the summer season and rather than return to the town to look for work, he decided to try to find some way of earning a living in the mountains. Neale and Dornan had worked several summers in the Tetons, Neale as guide and Dornan as a climbing ranger, and they suggested that Gary came with them.

The Tetons are a part of the Rockies in the state of Wyoming, to the south of Yellowstone National Park. They tower over the valley of Jackson Hole, which stretches out at two thousand metres above sea level, cut through by the Snake River and strewn with lakes. The landscape is dominated by the 4200-metre-high Grand Teton, the highest peak of the three - *Les Trois Tetons* - from which the massif gets its name. Once frequented by hunters and trappers - until the middle of the last century - the Snake River valley has gradually been taken over by ranchers who drove the herds of bison and elk towards the north. Jackson still resembles a cowboy town, despite the recent establishment of the National Park which is slowly changing the area's economy and thus its geographical features, replacing ranches with the accoutrements of tourism.

At that time, the area was going through a period of transition - the initial stages of tourism. The first hotels were being built in the town of Jackson, and a mountain guide service had been established in Moose. Contrary to the European alpine guide associations - which are made up of groups of professionally qualified mountaineers (established autonomously or under the direction of the alpine clubs in various countries, which in each case regulate the profession and supervise the appointment of guides) - in the United States, the companies which then offered guide services were commercial firms just like any other private service establishment. The Exum Mountain guide service in Moose was owned by Glen Exum, an alpinist who had opened several classic routes in the Tetons during the 1930s and who, for the past twenty years had offered his experience to the benefit of inexperienced or occasional alpinists. His Guide Service boasted a first-class staff. All the great American alpinists, at one point or another, had spent a summer in these mountains, and almost all of them had been employed by Exum for a season's work.

In America there was then no official body to issue guide licences. A guide was purely someone capable of accompanying a client in the mountains, guaranteeing them maximum safety, and was employed on the basis of his alpine curriculum vitae, or through introductions by guides or alpinists who could guarantee his reliability. He would no longer be a guide if he did not meet the standards required.

Gary was introduced to Exum by Sterling Neale. Before employing him, Exum put him to the test - as he did with all those who wanted to become guides - sending him out with a group of clients accompanied by expert

guides who would make a judgement of his capabilities
and the level of safety he could guarantee.

Between mountain trips Gary worked on repairing the roof
of the Guide Service building which had fallen in during
the winter. With him was another prospective guide, Bill
Briggs, a talented skier and a good climber despite a limp
brought about by a congenital hip defect. Nobody paid
attention to this defect, mostly because Bill was blessed
with a wonderful sense of humour and a good nature. Bill
was always conscious of his disability which he could forget
only when in the mountains or when he was playing and
singing the songs which had made him well-known as a
folk singer. Bill was fascinated by Gary, whose personality
intimidated him somewhat but whose ways amused him
greatly:

"Gary was big and had a threatening voice and
manners. He swore a lot, but in a humorous way, so it never
really 'grossed me out' as being objectionably vulgar. I never
could tell whether he was just trying to be vulgar or it was
really his way of communicating. Anyway it wasn't quite
him, so I always took it as a joke, thinking I was probably
laughing with him."

Gary was employed as a guide before Bill, which Bill took
as perfectly normal, considering that "Gary had an athletic
build while I was a cripple trying to compete with real
alpinists".

So Gary took up his job as a guide. Exum's guides
were stationed on the ´Guide's Hill´, near the start of the
path which led to the most popular routes. This area is a

beautiful spot beside Jenny Lake, popular with alpinists passing by who camp on the lake's banks. Some of those who come back each year have built wooden cabins.

Gary shared a tent with Barry Corbet, a talented Canadian alpinist just returned from an expedition to Mount McKinley in Alaska. This had been the first ascent of the South-west Rib of Mount McKinley, a breakthrough of staggering proportions for four young Americans - Bill Buckingham, Jake Breitenbach, Pete Sinclair and Barry Corbet. Corbet remembers Gary as "threatening at first, the sort of person whose self confidence was intimidating. He seemed lean and mean, a *méchant* image he cherished, as I found out later. He had a crew cut, was almost a caricature of the hotshot Californian rock-climber. I know now that we were intimidating ourselves, probably because we were sure he was going to turn out to be a much better climber than any of we Teton folks. What I mean is that I don't think there was anything mean in his character that we were perceiving - we were just projecting that upon him and somehow he encouraged our doing so. An element that WAS in his character was a bad temper. He was capable of completely losing control over small incidents, although he always directed his anger against inanimate objects rather than people. Sterling Neale told me of Gary's once beating the door of his old 1949 Ford with an ice axe."

Gary bought the old Ford with his income earned as a ´Snow Surveyor´ in the Sierra Nevada. He drove like a madman along the long, straight dirt track which led from Guide's Hill to Jackson Lake Lodge, regularly frightening the life out of his passengers. Bill had no car and always hitched a lift with Gary. They often went to the Lodge in Jackson, a saloon for tourists and cowboys, and often girls on holiday; while Gary would court, Bill would sit in a corner and play his banjo. Gary, who normally never drank alcohol, would easily get drunk on a couple of glasses and would start climbing up the walls in the bar, making use of the decorative stones for holds. And often the evening would end with them both being thrown out: Bill because of his banjo playing and Gary for his wall-climbing antics.

The two became inseparable and Gary, who was popular with the female sex, always tried to pick up two at a time - one for him and one for Bill. At the Teton Tea Parties, however, Bill made the most hits, with his songs and good nature. These parties took place round a bonfire on the banks of Jenny Lake, and the ´tea´ was of a particularly strong variety ... All the climbers and campers would join in, bringing drinks and food: they started up in the afternoon and would finish towards dawn, when everyone finally collapsed. Gary, normally Bill's ´big brother´ figure, felt left out when Bill charmed everyone with his music, and would resort to the most outrageous antics, like urinating on the fire, to shock everyone and draw attention back to himself.

Bill, on the other hand, even though he looked upon Gary and Barry Corbet as two semi-gods and his alpinist masters, went to great efforts to better them in notoriety - with first ascents and, in winter, reckless first ski-descents down faces which had previously only been descended by climbing - a forerunner of the extremes of modern skiing. Gary, in turn, encouraged Bill in all he did, but would get upset on those occasions when Bill was more brilliant than him: "One fall back then I joined Gary in Yosemite, California, to do a small climb or two. He wanted to put up a new route on the Pulpit - I think it was. Gary tried to get a piton in and swore a blue streak for half an hour, or more. Finally he let me try the lead and I was able to nest two pins in sidewise well enough to support my weight and allow me to use it for direct aid and complete the ascent. Gary was mad as hell: it was HIS route, etc. The anger was not directed at me, but at his failure."

There was a repressed rivalry between the two friends. If needed, they would have done anything for each other, but at the same time they kept an eye on each other like two fighting cocks tied a metre apart. And when they became rivals also in love, and Gary followed Bill and Judith all over Mexico, none of their friends from the Tetons were surprised. It was only logical that their friendship would result in melodrama.

And when Gary was found shot on the banks of Lake Jenny, ten years later on, those friends who would not accept the verdict of suicide - because they could not believe someone so full of life and spirit could kill himself - sought refuge in the old stories of rivalry and imagined an incident caused by some fight, or maybe even murder. This is how different versions of Gary's death were created, so difficult to unravel after so many years.

CHAPTER SEVEN

Pursuit Among the Volcanoes

Gary had met Judith in New York where he had found work as a private investigator for the Burns Detective Agency. Before taking on this new role, Gary had gone through several unsatisfactory jobs which he had thrown in after a few weeks: dance instructor in San Francisco, photo album seller in Oakland, used car salesman in Brooklyn, boy scout leader in Hell's Kitchen in the slums of New York City.

When he moved to the east coast, to Brooklyn, Gary was drawn to New York and all that it represented in history and culture. The western Americans have always had a kind of inferiority complex in relation to the east, at least until the recent post-beat culture and the rise of San Francisco as New York's cultural rival.

He left San Francisco by private aeroplane. How he managed this nobody knows. It was a small plane with wings of wood and cloth, recalls Steve Roper, who, with Bill Buckingham, had accompanied Gary to the airport. The small plane left the ground, and started circling, gaining more and more height, until it reached sufficient altitude to level out and disappear towards the east.

Gary was aware that he would miss the Sierra with its great mountains, but he was counting on continuing to climb. When climbing in the Tetons, he had met Fritz Wiessner, the famous German alpinist, turned American citizen. Wiessner had told Gary of climbing in the Shawangunks, an area not far from New York, and had introduced him to the American Alpine Club in New York.

Gary had always made good friends within the climbing groups he joined in the west. And if there were any climbers who were not too fond of him, for reasons of jealousy or simple difference of opinion and character, relationships would remain neutral. In the Gunks, Gary experienced for the first time difficulty in being accepted by the 'Vulgarians', the leading group in the area.

In addition his work did not exactly fulfil his restless spirit. After several changes he threw himself into the career of private detective, most probably picturing himself in some kind of thriller. However, he soon found himself stuck in the routines of a squalid employment: stalking unfaithful husbands and wives, gathering business information, investigation of overdue debts and cheques drawn on overdrawn accounts.

If he had not met Judith, Gary would have dropped everything and gone back to the west coast. They met at the Gunks, and after a few days Gary moved into her small apartment in Yorkville. For the first time in his life, Gary found himself putting the desire to stay with a woman in front of the longing for adventure, and for the first time - but not the last - he felt the fear of 'being trapped'. So he decided that Judith was immature and that she needed to live a little. He sent her off to the Tetons with a letter for Bill Briggs in which he asked him to help her, teach her the art of mountaineering and to show her ´how to find herself´. In contradiction to this act of separation, he promised Judith that when she returned they would get married and travel together to Europe, then a frequent dream of Gary's.

And so Judith left for the Tetons in the summer of 1959. Perhaps she was grateful to Gary for his efforts to help her find maturity, or maybe she was annoyed at his sending her away. And contrary to what Gary thought, she was probably not so immature. She understood that Gary did not want to get tied down, despite his promise of marriage. The fact was that she enjoyed Bill's company, and Bill took his task of helping her a little too seriously. Soon they were romantically involved, and everyone at Guide's Hill was aware of their feelings. Eventually, news of this reached Gary in New York.

At first, he did not believe it. It was too unbelievable that Judith would prefer Bill to him. Then he began to doubt his conviction, wrote ´the famous seventy page letter to Judith´, and prepared for his voyage to save his girl, just like some St. George setting off to rescue the princess from the dragon.

But in the meantime, Bill and Judith had travelled to Mexico with a friend, the folk musician Bob Coltman. They had planned this trip a while ago, and had discussed it with Sterling Neale and Charles Plummer, nicknamed 'Carlos', a climber of Mexican family who had offered them a bed at his parents' house in Mexico City. This was meant to be a climbing trip, but Bill decided to change his plans, and followed Coltman on a journey to ´collect recordings of popular Mexican music´. The truth of the matter was that he knew Gary was on his way, and did not want to wait around for him at Jackson Hole.

Sterling and Carlos were getting ready to leave also when Gary arrived from New York. They decided to travel together on a route which included climbing some of the snowcapped volcanoes in North Mexico and then travelling down to the south, to Acapulco. They were joined by 'Chief' Dunnagan, a Tetons Park ranger, and Pete Sinclair, just arrived from Alaska where he had climbed Mount McKinley and stayed for a year working as assistant for a *Life* photographer and as a park guardian.

The five of them left in two pick-ups, packed full with climbing gear and skis. They stopped in Colorado which had been dominated for several days by a blizzard. They took advantage of the storm to get in some skiing - the first time that season, and only at the start of October - and then they continued southwards.

Carlos was impatient to get to Mexico City to see his mother, but Gary and Dunnagan insisted on stopping at each village, ´to get to know the real Mexico´. For Gary, the truth was that he had no idea where Bill and Judith were, and in the absence of some better plan, he questioned everyone in the villages, hoping to find some trace of them. Sterling and Carlos wanted to climb some volcanoes, but Gary would not be dissuaded from his investigation of each village. Pete Sinclair, after twelve months of Alaskan snow and ice, was only too happy to back up Gary in postponing the climbing programme.

The group continued their travels from village to village, stopping off in bars and guest-houses, chatting with the locals. None of them spoke good Spanish, not even Carlos, who began to regret not having picked up the language as a boy. But they got by and had great fun like children on a school trip. They resembled a group of students, except for Gary who looked like a plundering Viking. His expressions, constantly changing with his moods, could have tremendous effects, and to make him look even more threatening, he had removed a false tooth, and swore that he would not put it back until he saw Judith again.

Often their visits to the bars would become nasty, as Gary tended to get aggressive after a few beers. In Ciudad Torreón, in a small crowded bar, a fight was in the air, and Pete Sinclair decided to slip a couple of Seconal tablets into Gary's beer. Gary did not see him do it, but at his first taste he realised - or maybe he was aware of it but wanted to pretend he could taste it. He flung the glass full of beer against the wall and grabbed the barman by his collar, lifting him up from behind the bar. "Three! I'll take three of you!" he roared, "Three against one!" He reckoned that with his size, it would not have been fair to take on only one small Mexican at a time. His friends struggled to calm him down, but their efforts did not succeed. Their last resort was to tie him up with climbing ropes, lift him like some bound salami sausage into the small pick-up and drive off as quickly as possible, before things exploded.

Once outside the town, they stopped to find a campsite and set him free. They were ready to face his wrath, but were surprised to see him walk off and settle down to sleep in a field of maize. They still swear that they heard him crying all night long.

And the next morning he joined the group again with his usual boyish smile.

The group continued their journey keeping a continuous watch on Gary, but encountering only a few minor scuffles. To keep out of trouble, they avoided brothels, as Gary had come to the conclusion that prostitutes should sleep with him purely because of his charm, and his pride would be hurt when they demanded payment. Finally, they arrived in Mexico City, where Carlos's mother, in between giving dancing lessons, took them on trips around the city and its surroundings.

By then, it was time to make some serious plans: Carlos suggested climbing two volcanoes, Ixtaccihuatl and Orizaba. But Gary had expected to find Bill and Judith in Mexico City and, in his disappointment, he wanted to press onwards. Pete, still feeling the snow and ice in his bones, voted to travel toward the south.

In a coastal village, Gary fell in love with some sixteen-year-old girl, six months pregnant. He wanted to help her, but as usual, in his role of white knight, he only managed to complicate matters and get into trouble. On this occasion, the girl went with Gary to his room, and the hotel owner, suspicious, lectured his friends on the respectability of his establishment, and threatened to throw them out if they had girls in their rooms. This presented a real problem. They had to get the girl out of Gary's room without the owner noticing, but he had positioned himself in the front porch, and refused to move. After several hours, the only solution was to resort to their ropes again. They secured the girl, pregnant and wearing high heels and a starched underskirt, and lowered her out of the window.

Once in Acapulco, they turned around and headed back to Mexico City, where they were greeted with the news that within one week, Bill, Judith and Bob would arrive. Finally Gary decided to stop his travels, and to climb Ixtaccihuatl, a 5,200-metre-high volcano.

Bill had telephoned to Carlos's mother to warn them of his arrival, and on the fateful day, Gary gave each of his friends a prearranged role. They were strategically positioned between the front door and the lounge, while Gary stood waiting in the hall, his arms folded, like some vengeful Aztec god. As Bill and Judith entered, the atmosphere became electric. But then, nothing happened. Bill hung his head in guilt before Gary, and when Gary tried to provoke him into fighting, Bill refused. Gary pushed him to the ground, but Bill did not fight back, and that was that. During all this, Judith stood with her eyes downcast, like some modest Madonna.

And then the discussions started and went on endlessly. First Gary and Bill went off to discuss the situation. When they came back Gary took Judith to one side, then Judith went off with Bill. As they were taking their time, Gary announced that he was going to search them out and if he found them behind a bush, he would impale them both on his ice-axe. Pete tried to calm him down by remarking that they were in the middle of a city, and that the closest bushes were some kilometres away. Finally, Bill and Judith came back, and Gary went off with Judith, then with Bill, and then again Bill with Judith ...

In the end, they decided that Judith should take the bus back to the States, while Bill would join Gary to climb Orizaba. Before taking leave of Judith, Gary wrote 'the famous twenty page letter to Judith's parents', giving instructions and advice on how to treat the girl. To help her or to punish her?

The more popular version of this story is that Gary fought Bill in Mexico City and made him see reason. This is not true. The four others present have told me the real story - Bill, Sterling, Carlos and Pete - and everything really did end up without violence. In fact, this happy ending was not liked by others and each embellished the tale.

Only Gary, Carlos and Sterling made it to the top of Orizaba, the third highest mountain in North America. Bill and the others, exhausted by recent events and the altitude, turned back half way.

At the Mexican border, on their way back to the States, they had already passed customs when Pete, who had a bad headache which numerous aspirin had not cured, took a small bottle of codeine from the first-aid kit. A young, zealous customs officer noticed this and demanded: "What is that?" They told him. "What else do you have?" In the face of a search, they announced: "Seconal and morphine". The word 'morphine' produced an immediate reaction. Their luggage was searched thoroughly. The customs officers telephoned the American General Attorney and the doctor who had given Carlos the morphine prescription - for the emergency team at Dartmouth Mountaineering Club.

But the one thing that most aroused the customs officers' suspicions were Gary's diaries - four thick volumes each page crammed with handwriting. In the diaries, Gary had not just told of their journeys, but also given vent to his emotions and anger. The language was not exactly fitting and the officer in charge regarded these as more suspicious than the morphine.

There then followed thorough interrogations. The American District Attorney finally decided not to incriminate the five, once it was established that they were not drug smugglers. But then the officer in charge called Gary into his office, and asked him who Judith was. Gary refused to talk. If that was not bad enough, Gary had written in his diaries about two books he had borrowed from Pete: *Tropic of Cancer* and *Tropic of Capricorn* by Henry Miller, banned in the United States for reasons of obscenity. Finally, they were allowed to go, but under threat of a pending trial, and Sterling´s VW van was impounded. They had to stop off in Texas and find some work in order to get the van back and pay the trial fees. The four volumes of Gary's diary were kept by the customs officers.

Looking back, Pete believes that the two Miller books were a crucial factor in Gary's decision to go to France.

At Xochimilico, near Mexico City. Left to right: "Chief" Dunnigan, Mrs Evely Plummer, Pete Sinclair, ano, ano, ano, Sterling Neale (with picnic box), Gary Hemming at front (with missing tooth).   Photo: "Carlos" Plummer.

Gary Hemming (left) and Sterling Neale approaching the summit of Pico de Orizaba, 18,896 ft.
Photo: "Carlos" Plummer.

Bill Briggs in the Cascade Range, Washington State, c.1958. Photo: Barry Corbet.

Gary Hemming (left) en route to the Calanques. Photo: George Collouilet.

Gary Hemming on the *Walker Spur*, Grandes Jorasses. Photo: Henry Kendall.

Gary Hemming (left) and John Harlin with their gear at the Envers des Aiguilles refuge.
Photo: Tom Frost.

Gary Hemming on the *South Face* of the Aiguille du Fou. Photo: Tom Frost.

Gary Hemming leading on the *South Face* of the Aiguille du Fou. Photo: Tom Frost.

Barry Corbet on Mt. Tyree, 16,290 ft. (first ascent), Antarctica, 1967. Photo: John Evans.

Grand Teton from the south. Photo: Donald Bennet.

Jenny Lake. Photo: Donald Bennet.

Gary Hemming (near the end of the road) in Alaska, 1969. Photo: Denny Wilk.

CHAPTER EIGHT

The Old Continent

In Texas, Gary decided that he no longer wanted to return to New York, and stopping to work was an opportunity to postpone his return. They took temporary jobs on a construction site for a pipeline, and when the project was completed and his friends travelled home, Gary stayed in the south looking for different jobs. In New Orleans he found work on a prawn trawler, and spent several months in the Gulf of Mexico. Then he lingered some time in Tampa picking fruit, but finally decided to head for home, in San Diego. He had finally decided to stop wasting time, and to carry out his project to travel to Europe.

At Christmas John Harlin had written to say that he was leaving for a five-year stint with the USAF in Germany. John had managed to get a pilot's licence during his years at University. He had married at twenty years of age and by then was twenty four and had two children. Living off climbing and adventure was not easy with a family, but John nurtured a dream of returning to the Alps. He longed to climb the north face of the Eiger, which he had attempted four years earlier. The Eiger is in the Bernese Oberland, and its north face is one of the most dangerous in the Alps - because of a combination of technical difficulty, rock falls and sudden storms, it had seen many deaths before being conquered in 1938. Many of those trying to repeat the ascent fall victim to the vagaries of the face, and an attempt alone carries an implication of great courage.

On his first attempt, John had chosen the wrong company - Tenzing Norkay, the Sherpa who had accompanied Hillary on the first ascent of Everest in 1953, and who was at that time in Switzerland for several conferences. John had chosen him because of his name, and Tenzing had accepted, maybe out of curiosity. But Tenzing was not a north face man, and grew impatient with John, a young, ambitious climber with half his years and experience, who tried to teach him complicated rope manoeuvres. They climbed the Jungfrau by the normal route and after studying the Eiger from the west ridge, they separated. Then John took up his assignment with the Air Force, and moved to the NATO base in Hahn, on the Rhine. Before leaving with his wife and children, he wrote to Gary, "We are expecting you".

Back in the States, Gary had to earn money for his trip, and for his keep in Europe for the first few months. He had decided to become a student and had chosen France because he wanted to learn French and be close to the Alps. He managed to get a student grant for the University of Grenoble, and finally left in November 1960.

Grenoble is a beautiful city at the foot of the Vercors massif, and close to Savoie and the Mont Blanc massif. Its University is in the old part of the town, situated on a rock above the river. This was the Europe Gary had always dreamed of, the city's walls and buildings witness to centuries of history and culture. He had to learn French quickly so that he could communicate, and he made all kinds of plans. Most important of these was to work towards realising his twin dream: becoming a writer and a great alpinist. Whilst dreaming of bigger things, he kept fit on the mountains surrounding the city.

There is a low-lying crag just outside Grenoble, and it was here that he met Claude. She was one year older than Gary and was at that time developing an interest in climbing. She came from a Protestant family and lived alone in Grenoble, where she was a teacher. Her command of English was good, and this helped their relationship develop, as Gary was taking longer than expected to learn his new language. Gary was fascinated by Claude's grace and independence, and as he got to know her better, he also appreciated her intelligence and culture, even though he would often proclaim, "Oh, you're nothing but an intellectual pain in the neck!"

Gary moved in with Claude in rented rooms in the old town, and this marked the start of a period of stability, unusual for Gary. He was very happy with Claude, whose independent way of life did not make him feel 'trapped', as he had with Judith in New York. They lived in the same house but both lived their own lives without feeling restricted by the other. Gary went to University, studied, trained and wrote - wrote a lot. Claude gave constant encouragement, without making her presence felt. She also had her own studies, interests and her own group of friends. Sometimes she would go with Gary to the mountains, but more often than not would wait for him at home. She enjoyed the mountains, but they were not her overriding passion, and she would never be a real alpinist.

Gary got to know people and made friendships. His closest friends were the Thomas brothers, good alpinists, and Georges Collombat, a 'pied noir', as the French call the expatriates from the Northern African colonies, who came back to France from Algeria after the war of independence. Georges was a young, sensitive boy with poor health and the soul of a mystic, consumed with nostalgia for the sunny places of his childhood, for which he found consolation in the mountains. Gary grew fond of him, and developed a protective role towards him.

The next few years were intense ones for Gary - climbing in the Alps, studying, writing. Much of his time was spent on writing a book on Californian climbing. He wanted to write this in French so that he could have his work published in France, and this required endless rewriting. During this time he wrote often to John Harlin, whom he also visited in Bernkastel, in the Moselle valley, where John had moved to avoid the stifling environment of a military base. On arriving, Gary surveyed with suspicion the comforts of John's house: the air conditioning, household machines, children's toys. To Gary, marriage was a trap, into which John had fallen. Luckily for John, Gary was there to pull him out: "Let's pull something off together. A really big project, important. What do you say?"

At that time, space exploration was a new but developing science, and Gary had played with the idea of installing a 'high altitude space laboratory´ on one of the

Himalayan peaks. The laboratory would in fact be a centre for advanced training of astronauts, for high altitude would provide the perfect introduction to the conditions involved in space travel. John was immediately interested in the project and they both worked separately on this for some time, while keeping each other up to date with their progress. The laboratory was to be installed on K2, the second highest mountain after Everest. Of course, they had to elicit the involvement of the American Government, and with this support they were to combine the project of the new laboratory with an expedition to ascend K2, which had never been climbed by Americans. The expedition would of course be led by Gary and John. Naturally, the idea of the laboratory was purely an excuse to make an attempt on K2, but both Gary and John eventually developed a serious interest in the project's scientific aspect. John compiled a very detailed report, which was subsequently verified by a physiologist involved in space projects and who served in the Air Force. Even the Commandant of the base in Hahn wrote an official letter of recommendation to the Washington Office of Bioastronomy. John was sure that he would soon get the chance to travel to Washington, to meet with important generals, maybe even with the Defence Secretary, McNamara.

In the meantime, Gary had been busy with the climbing part of the project. He had maintained correspondence with his American friends, and wrote of the project to Willi Unsoeld, whom he had met in the Tetons. Unsoeld was a Himalayan veteran: his first expedition was to Nanda Devi as far back as 1953, and his experience and knowledge made him an essential character to involve in the project.

However, Unsoeld showed some reserve. Although the principal idea of a high-altitude training centre for astronauts was accepted as a good one, K2 was not the ideal mountain, because of the difficult approach and the ever present danger of avalanches. He suggested they select some area more easy to reach, maybe even by plane or helicopter. Also he advised them to be aware of political problems, and that they would be better off avoiding, for example, areas near the Tibetan border. As for the K2 expedition, that was a splendid idea; but it had nothing to do with the space laboratory. The astronauts would definitely benefit from training at high altitude, coping with lack of oxygen and severe physical and psychological conditions, but Unsoeld could not understand what benefit they would gain from the presence of the climbers. He concluded that they would be better advised to divide the project into two, and proceed with each separately.

Despite his opinions, Unsoeld did provide Gary with useful addresses and information on what climbing gear they should procure for the expedition. He would not be taking part, as he had already been invited on an expedition to Everest, in what was to be the first American expedition to reach the highest summit in the world, in 1963.

Gary was still determined to go ahead with the original project, but despite all John's efforts their project never reached the desk of anyone important enough to take the necessary decisions, and eventually it was forgotten.

So Gary and John decided to drop their grandiose ideas

and aim for something more modest, more practical. They planned to spend the summer of 1961 climbing together, and prepared a list of routes. This was to be Gary's first real season in the Alps, and he was very excited about it. However, living and climbing with John turned out to be difficult. This was not so surprising given that both had such strong characters - two natural leaders who could not bear being told what to do.

The first signs of trouble began to show in March, when Gary was staying with John in his house. He had been there one week, with the intention of climbing with John, but had hurt his foot and had to cancel their plans. John was not lenient with Gary. Because of him, he had missed an opportunity to go climbing, and he made his feelings known.

That summer, they spent most of their time in the Mont Blanc massif, pitching their little tent on the glacier or in the valley, arguing when they could not go climbing due to bad weather, arguing even when they were climbing. John was the snow and ice expert between them, and would grow impatient with Gary, not so experienced on such terrain. Gary was often subjected to cruel jokes about his performance. On the other hand, Gary was very adept at artificial climbing, despite his promotion of free climbing. On several occasions, for example, once on the east face of the Grand Capucin, John became very confused with the ropes, and Gary did not hesitate to launch into a pedantic lecture on this subject, which infuriated John.

For all July the weather was poor. Gary and John completed few ascents. Often they had to turn back half way up the

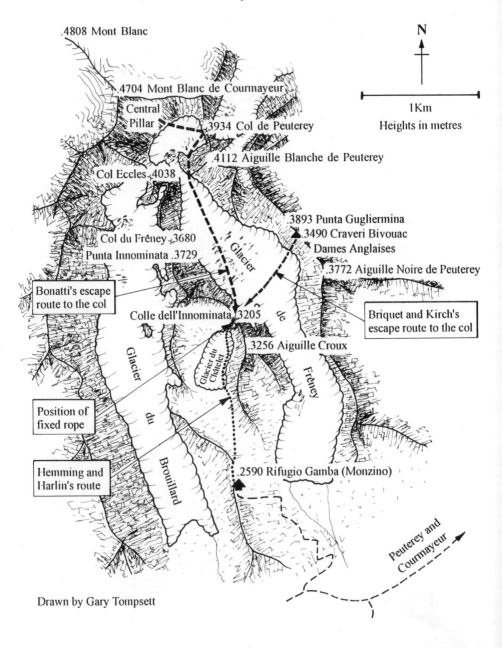

The Frêney face of Mont Blanc

.4808 Mont Blanc

.4704 Mont Blanc de Courmayeur

Central Pillar

.3934 Col de Peuterey

.4112 Aiguille Blanche de Peuterey

Col Eccles .4038

.3893 Punta Gugliermina

.3490 Craveri Bivouac

Dames Anglaises

Col du Frêney .3680

Punta Innominata .3729

.3772 Aiguille Noire de Peuterey

Glacier

| Bonatti's escape route to the col |

Colle dell'Innominata .3205

| Briquet and Kirch's escape route to the col |

Glacier du Châtelet

.3256 Aiguille Croux

Glacier

du

Frêney

de

| Position of fixed rope |

Brouillard

| Hemming and Harlin's route |

.2590 Rifugio Gamba (Monzino)

Peuterey and Courmayeur

N

1Km

Heights in metres

Drawn by Gary Tompsett

mountain, and after one such day on the south ridge of the Aiguille Noire de Peuterey, when they had been hit by a sudden blizzard, they decided not to waste any more time and to return to Germany. In the valley it was raining and the chances of the weather changing for the better seemed distant.

Just as they were taking down their tent, however, they learned that two young men, who had been camping near them and had set off to climb the Punta Gugliermina, had been missing for a few days. These were Henri Briquet, a Swiss , and a German by the name of Konrad Kirch. The girlfriend of one of the two men had notified the rescue service, and two guides had arrived from Courmayeur. However, two men alone could do little with all the snow that had fallen. What to do? Gary and John would often argue about the smallest things, but in this case they did not hesitate and climbed back up to the Rifugio Gamba to offer their help. However, the welcome they received from the two guides and the guardian of the rifugio was far from warm as though they were intruders. Despite this, they stayed. They were told that a rescue team from Courmayeur should be on its way, and only if they did not arrive could Gary and John be put to use. Fortunately, the rescue team turned up and the Americans were about to go down, when they were met by a group of five Frenchmen, soaked to the skin: four French climbers were trapped on the Central Pillar of Frêney.
"Who are they?"
"Guillaume, Vieille and two others." The two others were Mazeaud and Kohlman.
"God, we know Guillaume and Vieille. On the Central Pillar

of Frêney! That was on our list of routes."

This climb had in fact been part of their plan. It was the last unclimbed pillar on the south face of the Mont Blanc massif, and climbers from all over Europe were caught up in the race to make the first ascent. Apparently there were also three Italians trapped with the French. One of these was the great Alpinist Walter Bonatti, and with him were two of his most competent companions, Oggioni, and the Milanese Gallieni.

Rain continued to fall, and the Frenchmen decided to eat, sleep and then the next day climb the Aiguille Croux to view the climbers' position with binoculars. And what about the guides? "There is nothing we can do. It is too difficult." They would also wait until the next day when they would maybe climb to the Col Eccles to see what they could do.

Gary and John decided to go with the Frenchmen to the Aiguille Croux, from where they could also see the Punta Gugliermina. Would the other two lads still be alive? Three of the guides would go and look for them the following day.

But next day the snow was still falling. The guides walked outside the hut, decided, "It's snowing," and went back to bed. Gary and John became more and more furious. Eventually they all got up, but the Frenchmen had changed their plans: they would go to the Col Eccles with the guides. However, Gary and John decided to keep to their original plan to climb Aiguille Croux, and on the way there, they came across three figures descending the snow-covered slopes. It was the three guides who were supposed to be rescuing the two young men missing on the Punta

Gugliermina. Were they giving up? Gary and John decided to take their place, to go to the help of the Swiss and German. They thought this over and came to the conclusion that since the Frenchmen on the Pillar were accompanied by such a great climber as Bonatti they had nothing to fear. Bonatti knew the Mont Blanc massif so well that they had probably already managed to descend.

So they returned to the hut and told the guardian of their plans; that they would try to reach the bivouac at the 'Dames Anglaises' , a minuscule corrugated-metal hut where the two may have sought refuge. The guardian advised them to go via the Colle dell'Innominata. Gary and John were surprised by this advice as they had seen the guides descending much lower down.

"Isn't it better to go that way?"

"No, no. There are far too many crevasses in that area. They only went there to look up through their binoculars. They're sure to be back soon."

So John and Gary set off for the Colle dell'Innominata, a gap between the Punta Innominata and the Aiguille Croux. Their climb was difficult due to the continual snowfall: John's experience was put to the test. On arriving at the col, he shouted down to Gary: "I'm up - climb!" To his surprise he heard a distant voice responding from the Punta Gugliermina. The two lads! They were alive!

Alone John and Gary were unable to do anything. They quickly descended, fixing a 50-metre rope from a peg on the col and returned to the hut to find some help.

"Too much snow." No one was willing to help them.

"How can you just sit there? They're alive, but they'll be very weak after five days. We can't help them alone. There's too much snow for two, but if there were ten or twenty of us we could take it in turns to kick steps up the Frêney glacier towards them ... "

Nobody moved and eventually Briquet and Kirch found their way back alone. During all this time they had been in the Craveri Bivouac at the 'Dames Anglaises', and although weak, they were able to move. Hearing voices from the col, and a clearing in the weather, had encouraged them to take on the descent. Then the fixed rope left by Gary and John below the Colle dell'Innominata resolved the problems they would have had with the difficult fifty metres.

They were exhausted and had symptoms of frostbite, so Gary and John decided to help them down to the valley. The rifugio was full with rescue team guides and there were not enough beds. And besides, Gary was so furious with the guides for refusing to accompany him and John on an attempt to help the seven on the Central Pillar, that things were growing rather tense. They would be better off leaving. "They can't just sit there doing nothing. They must do something sooner or later."

But none of them moved. And so the seven climbers trapped on the pillar had to attempt the descent without help. The weather grew continually worse and conditions were extremely difficult. Four of the climbers died from exposure. Only Bonatti, Mazeaud and Gallieni survived. They also made use of Gary and John's fixed rope below the Colle dell'Innominata. Thinking that the rescue team had placed the rope, they wondered why they had not placed it on the more difficult north side, which would have considerably reduced a long ascent and, maybe, avoided such a tragic conclusion.

CHAPTER NINE

Summer on Mont Blanc

Gary and John's parting that summer was a bitter one. They had had a disappointing climbing season and relationships between the two had remained tense throughout. An entry in Gary's diary reads "Indeed we came as close as two people can come to killing one another from sheer hate and frustration with the other". In truth they knew that they were a brilliant team in the mountains despite their excessively strong personalities creating an insurmountable barrier. Their arguments continued and the two of them grew into the embodiment of the typical love-hate relationship which can unite such great rivals. They still sought each other out, as Gary could not imagine any project without John, and John could not imagine going to the mountains without Gary.

After that summer, Gary climbed with his French friends in the Vercors and on the Calanques, an area of limestone cliffs towering over the sea, along the coast between Toulon and Marseilles. While climbing here, Gary missed having a climbing companion of John's standard and wrote to him: "Why don't you come to Calanques?"

Between climbing and lectures at the University, Gary found time for some small jobs, in order to earn money for his travels to the mountains. He remained with Claude, but as they had come to a mutual agreement not to invade the other's space, and as Claude's apartment was rather small, he moved temporarily into a large villa which he shared with three other students. The Thomas brothers had set up a small forge nearby where they produced pitons and other climbing aids and Gary developed a great interest in the manufacture of such gear. In California he had followed the experiments of Yvon Chouinard and Tom Frost who had together invented technical equipment of real genius, among which was the RURP (realized ultimate reality piton). This was a thin blade of steel made to fit into narrow, shallow cracks and still hold the weight of one person. The RURP had been instrumental in the ascent of some pitches on great routes in Yosemite, where Chouinard and Frost had opened new routes with Robbins and Pratt.

Gary wrote often to Chouinard, presenting technical problems and climbing projects to him. He wrote of his enthusiasm for the Alps. That is where real climbing is, he would say, completely different from climbing in California.

"Honest there is no comparison between mountain climbing or rock climbing in the States and true unadulterated alpine climbing. It's 10 times more dangerous, 10 times more exhausting. You are just never safe. Every single step is dangerous. From the time you leave the valley till you return the mental pressure alone is exhausting enough. Added to this though is the fact that you're almost always between 10,000 and 15,000 feet, almost always carrying packs of 30 to 40 lbs. on your back, almost always in a hurry because of the weather or the approaching darkness, always cold or damp or hungry, or all three."

He invited Chouinard to join him in the Alps, to climb with him. If money was a problem, he would put him up. Four ascents which he would like to climb with Chouinard were foremost in Gary's mind: the north face of the Eiger, the Central Pillar of Frêney, the Walker Spur on the Grandes Jorasses and the west face of the Dru.

The Pillar of Frêney had already been climbed by three Englishmen and a Pole [10], followed by two ropes of French and Italians [11], only a few weeks after the tragic descent of Bonatti and his companions. Gary and John had attempted the route after them, but during one of the first pitches there was a rock fall, Gary was hit on the head and they had to turn back. However, they did not immediately return to the valley because, that very same day, a military aircraft had flown into the cables of the téléphérique in the Vallée Blanche, which stretch across the Mont Blanc massif from Punta Helbronner to the Aiguille du Midi. This accident had caused the cables to snap, and numerous cable cars holding tourists had fallen onto the glacier. There was a number of deaths, and there was great urgency to rescue those injured as they could not be left too long in the icy conditions on the glacier. Rescue teams from France and Italy arrived promptly but there were not enough people, and so Gary, despite suffering from severe headaches, did

[10]   C.J.S. Bonington, I.Clough, D.Whillans and J.Djyclosz

[11]   R. Desmaison, Y. Pollet-Villard, P.Julien and I. Piussi

not hesitate in joining John to help in the rescue.

The Walker Spur is a very severe route on the north face of the Grandes Jorasses. This mountain is part of the watershed for the Mont Blanc massif and its north face dominates the Leschaux glacier. The spur was climbed for the first time in 1938 by a team of Italians led by Riccardo Cassin. Since then, only twenty or so repeat ascents had been made.

Gary had studied all the available literature needed for a ´topo´ - the term used by the French for a route description - and had been on several reconnoitring trips to study the route more closely. In addition, he had attempted a snow and ice ascent with John the previous winter - this was to be the first winter ascent - but they had to turn back after having climbed only a third of the route.

In the summer of 1962, Henry Kendall, an old friend who had been with Gary and John on the expedition to the Battle Range in the Selkirks in Canada, arrived in France. He was a physicist working as a researcher in the Massachusetts Institute of Technology at Cambridge, in the States, and had been transferred to France for several months to work in an electronics laboratory in Orsay. Once in France, he tracked down Gary, and joined him at Chamonix in August. They climbed a couple of routes, enjoying each other's company, and, in continued glorious weather, decided to make an attempt on the Walker. They were not alone on the route, several other parties taking advantage of the good weather, but after only a small number of pitches, as is typical of the weather on the Mont Blanc, they found themselves surrounded by a thick fog.

All the parties descended successfully, despite numerous rock falls, and after seven hours Gary and Henry reached the foot of the route.

Three days later, they were ready to make a fresh attempt, and this time they had the route to themselves. They bivouacked after having climbed almost half of the most difficult pitches, and the following day, in brilliant weather, they reached the top. Theirs was the first American ascent of the Walker, and when Kendall returned to the States to tell of their achievement, the news was published in all the climbing clubs' bulletins and made quite an impression.

That same season, Gary had already realised another of his alpine dreams - the Dru, one of the most beautiful pillars in the Mont Blanc massif. In the previous summer, he had made a couple of attempts with John on the most difficult route, the Bonatti Pillar on the Petit Dru, but this was one of the several routes they had had to abandon due to poor weather. However, during these attempts, Gary had noticed the smoothness of the west face. This had been climbed by only one route, opened in 1952 by four French guides, one of whom, Guido Magnone, wrote a book, *The West Face*, entirely devoted to the first ascent. The Magnone route initially follows a couloir and is characterised by rock falls in its lower reaches. Gary had the initiative to trace a direct route, from the foot of the rock face vertically to the highest parts of the Magnone route, to the famous ´jammed block´, below the 90-metre dihedral which leads to the fateful pendulum; so critical for the rescue four years later.

That summer, Royal Robbins, the king of Yosemite,

was also in Chamonix. Gary and he had met in California, at Tahquitz Rock, but had never climbed together. Gary had great admiration for Robbins, and told him of his project. In July, after three days on the face, they accomplished the *American Direct*, then the most aesthetic and difficult route in the Mont Blanc massif.

Gary's admiration for Royal Robbins was not only for his climbing exploits on the great Yosemite faces, but also for his ethical vision of climbing. On numerous occasions, Robbins had said "It doesn't matter what route you climb, but the way you climb it"; declarations which had been debated and which eventually led the way for the modern appreciation of free climbing. Gary did not totally reject the idea of artificial climbing; he would in fact experiment with and test out new techniques and gear involved in artificial methods. However, he agreed with Robbins that these aids should be used solely to overcome extremely difficult pitches which could not be climbed otherwise, and which presented barriers to achieving fine new routes: artificial aids should not be used as the only means to complete a route from start to finish. This view reiterated the ideals of traditional alpinism, which had almost become obsolete by the 60s, at a time when all the major routes in the Alps had been climbed, and maximum difficulty was then sought by taking the most direct route, following a maxim that originated from the great Italian pioneer, Comici: "I wish someday to make a route and from the summit let fall a drop of water and this is where my route will have gone".

When opening the *American Direct* on the Dru,

Hemming and Robbins made use of technically advanced pitons and gear, produced in the States. In 1962, these were only available in America, and Europe lay far behind. It is possible that, without these aids and the associated refined techniques, tested out on the sheer walls in Yosemite, the *American Direct* would not have been climbed at that time. But the line of the route, perfectly direct, has the logic and beauty of the great, classical ascents.

Three years later, Robbins and John Harlin opened a new route, the *'American extreme direct'* (known as *American Direttissima*) between the Magnone route and the Bonatti Pillar. This ascent was even more daring and travelled more vertically up from the base, than the route opened in '62, but Hemming and Robbins' 'Direct' remained the route which attracted most admiration and was the most coveted of all the routes on the west face of the Dru.

CHAPTER TEN

Lolita

That summer of 1962, with its alpine achievements, represented the end of a unique but short period of peace of mind for Gary.

In August of 1962, he joined E.N.S.A., the national school for skiing and alpinism in Chamonix, as ´Auditeur Libre´ (unregistered student attending lectures). This is where mountain guides receive their training and it is a highly prestigious school. Gary had still not overcome his problems when climbing on snow and was particularly interested in learning techniques on mixed ground - rock and snow - and on glaciers; the use of crampons and ice-axe, cutting steps in the glacier, safety on glaciers and on fresh snow slopes. He lacked so many techniques in this regard, which had led to frustration when he was climbing with John.

Soon, however, Gary knew it all. In fact, he learned so quickly that he began to argue with the instructors, making pedantic comments such as, "I think this way is better", and then launching into long-winded explanations. Unfortunately, he was often right, and this did not earn the instructors' affections. At that time, Gary had a rather long and untidy beard and wore his hair down to his shoulders. He was hardly a model of elegance: he owned one pair of jeans for days in town, one pair of breeches for climbing, and one jumper - the infamous red jumper. This was his wardrobe, which he washed and patched until they were threadbare.

At E.N.S.A., appearances were important. René Desmaison, an instructor in the school in 1960, recalls: "In the climbing school, and according to the head instructor, to climb in shorts and T-shirt, as we did at Fontainbleau, would have been shameful. We were guide instructors! Noblesse oblige! Appearances were utmost. The uniform of a real guide was de rigueur: grey trousers, grey jumper with badges, boots and wool socks (the uniform of that time). ... I have never seen Armand Charlet without breeches and beret, whether he was climbing or in town ..."

It is strange that no one commented on Gary's clothes right from the start. But after a couple of weeks, and as Gary was beginning to cause irritation with his comments and with his popularity because of his ascents, the director of the course summoned him and commanded him to assume a ´decent image´. To start with, Gary had to shave and cut his hair. Gary refused, and was expelled from the course.

During this period - a period of elation because of his successful ascent and of depression due to his expulsion from the course - Gary met Marie in the Bar National.

Normally Gary did not go to bars, but the National was the noisy meeting point for English-speaking climbers, and Gary found their company preferable to the French, even though he had made friends with some young climbers from Chamonix.

Marie was a thin, terrified-looking girl with smooth, dark hair and a fringe which came down to her eyes, intensifying her childish looks. Gary was attracted by her fragile figure and her apparent need for protection. Marie could not keep from staring at Gary's lanky figure and his smiling eyes as he approached her. He spoke gently to her: Gary could express a mixture of strength and tenderness, and with this he won her over. By the end of the evening, she left with him for his tent. Gary fell head over heels in love with this childish girl, but was never to know whether Marie loved him or not.

Claude recalls: "It was a typical 60s love story. You can't really understand what happened if you haven't read a book that was very popular then - Lolita. Marie was a Lolita. When they met, Gary was in his thirties, and she was seventeen years old. But the difference in age was not the only reason I would call her a Lolita. Her behaviour, and most of all her appearance - small and fragile - made her perfect for the character. Those were the years of the great prima donna, like Sylvie Vartan. The female model was as thin as a rake, like Twiggy. Marie was a bit of both, the woman-child, and Gary was fascinated by her. But most of all, Gary fell in love with Marie because she represented the most popular values of those times: in particular anti-conformism, manifested as a kind of rebellion. So if you look at Gary and Marie with that background, their love story was a kind of forerunner for 1968."

Claude's judgement of Marie's character echoes the high esteem Gary had for the girl during the long time he spent in love with her. Apart from a few, unique moments of lucidity, Gary saw Marie through rose-coloured spectacles, mistaking her schoolgirl immaturity for reserve, and her stubbornness for rebellion. He was convinced that Marie had the same vocation, the same desire for adventure, and he dreamed of travelling the world over with Marie at his side.

"But Marie was a serious student, and was determined to finish her school." Looking back now, after all those years, Claude feels the hurt of more painful wounds than those of jealousy, and she can think of Marie with understanding: "When she was finished with school, she registered in the Philosophy faculty at University. Now I don't really think of philosophy as being incompatible with a sense of adventure, but Gary saw it that way. He could not comprehend her hesitation to follow him to the ends of the earth, no delay. Gary's failure to understand this made their love story impossible."

In truth, their story finished much earlier than is believed, though Gary tormented Marie with hundreds of letters, begging her to leave with him. They first met while she was on holiday in her parents' villa in Les Houches, near Chamonix, and maybe at the start she did fall in love with Gary, the American who was so different from the people of her middle-class family environment. Marie was the daughter of a Sorbonne professor and had a sister a few years older. The family was well off: they had a house in Fonteney, near Paris, one in Les Houches, and another by the sea, near Marseilles. Marie was just like many other girls, an average student and rather quiet. But just like other seventeen-year-old girls, she boasted of a pretended rebellion against her parents when she was out. She would spend the winter in Paris and the summer travelling between their house by the sea and that in the mountains. Maybe she did fall in love with Gary, but at the end of that summer in 1962 there was a nasty scene the evening before she returned to Paris, caused by some silly argument, and she no longer wanted anything to do with this older man, who frightened her with the intensity of his feelings.

But she would never quite break things completely with Gary. Deep down it must have been quite exciting to receive burning love letters from a grown man, a fascinating stranger - too exciting maybe to give it all up. She would never say definitely ´no´, and had Gary constantly running after her. She would agree to meet him in Paris, in London when she travelled there with her family, in Marseilles, in Chamonix. Gary would come running but she would often not turn up. On other occasions she would meet him but with a resigned air which Gary interpreted as some internal torment. And Marie would always find some excuse to run off again, just as she had rekindled Gary's passion for her, keeping it as taut as a violin string.

This episode would make Gary seem ridiculous had it not been for the fact that he was sincerely convinced of the greatness of his love and of the importance of ´saving´ Marie from the middle-class environment in which she was trapped. His love must indeed have been great if it prevented him from seeing the truth, but Gary seemed to have a constant need to be possessed by a great but impossible love. The truth is that only an impossible love can remain ideally perfect and unchanged by the passage of time. No woman of flesh and blood could compare to the ideal woman Gary needed. And so Gary's most intense love affairs were with women he could not have, or those he had had and lost, like Marie.

Gary wrote constantly to Marie, and for years filled his diary with fantastic dreams of how life would be with Marie; travels with Marie when she would finally decide to go with him; expectations and regrets.

At the end of summer, he also left Chamonix and went back to Claude. And in fact a true forerunner of the dramatic social change in 1968 is the relationship between Gary and Claude. Gary told Claude about Marie - obviously about the idealised version he had created for himself. Naturally Claude was jealous, and this news hurt her, but she stuck solidly to her principles of respect for individual freedom, which she had discussed so often with Gary, and she hid her feelings. She did not pretend to ignore what had happened just to keep Gary, but spoke openly about the situation. They also discussed their relationship and agreed that it was too important to throw away. However, Gary was in no doubt that if Marie came back to him and wanted to live with him, he would not be able to share his love between the two. This was a hard fact for Claude to accept, but she felt very strongly about Gary, and his freedom had almost become a point of honour for her. Claude decided to take on a role of lover-friend, a part she would remain faithful to forever.

While waiting for Marie to come back to him, Gary lived from day to day, moving around and taking different jobs. He went to England to meet Marie in London, and then travelled to the north to work on a road-building site. During this period, he took advantage of his location to visit the Lake District, meet some English climbers and go rock-climbing. He had also started writing to John again, who had been transferred to Garmisch in the Bavarian Alps. Gary went to visit him there, and stayed for a while, working on the installation of ski lifts in a ski centre.

CHAPTER ELEVEN

An Important Year

Eventually Gary returned to Grenoble and Claude, and started his University course again. His relationship with Claude was marked by maximum fairness: they shared the rent and other daily living costs equally, and respected their mutual privacy. They were two good friends, and had been since they met, but they also had strong feelings for each other which Marie's role had not caused to fade. When Gary was not troubled by imminent meetings with Marie, their life together was tranquil.

However, after a few months, their relationship was put to the test by an important event: Claude was pregnant. This could have caused Gary to panic. He had always been terrified of being trapped by a woman, and for Claude this could have been the opportunity to tie Gary down, snatching him from Marie's clutches. But neither of them viewed it in this way. Gary was elated about the idea of being a father, while Claude immediately addressed the problem of how to combine the baby's need for a father, with the certain absence of Gary. The last thing she wanted was for Gary to stay with her out of a sense of duty towards the baby.

At that time Claude was studying for her exams and working, while Gary was following his University course, going to the mountains and working on his book on Californian climbing. They discussed this situation in the rational manner that they talked about other moral, social and political issues. The problem of responsibility was a subject they had discussed many times, and the decisions they took were based on the principles they had always maintained.

From a practical point of view, the problem was soon resolved. Financially Gary would share the child's needs with Claude, who had a regular job and therefore could manage. The child would take its father's surname, because this was proper, and because both Claude and Gary wanted it to be called Hemming. The child would remain with Claude: Gary could not imagine a better upbringing for his child. And when Gary left - and it was understood that he would leave, either with Marie or alone - the child would obviously lose the value of his constant presence, but Gary would visit them as often as possible, and would keep in touch with Claude so they could discuss practical problems that might arise, and in particular to take part in important decisions regarding his child.

Gary and Claude's relationship would remain the same, affectionate and open, but they would be free to enter into other emotional relationships just as openly. In theory and practice, this was a forerunner of the experimental ´open relationships´ of the 70s. The decision to escape from unacceptable ties but still maintain his responsibilities gave

Gary great joy:

"... I've fallen certainly on a woman of remarkable qualities and in the long run this returns to her. This very bad turn with Marie was a stroke of the finest ... For us to become married would be to turn our relationship that is beginning to become something, into mediocrity. We now make ourselves something special, something different than those about us. We are not just an ordinary pair of unhappy creatures obviously thrown together by the bad luck of having a child at the wrong time - we are apart from this and we each carry a cross of some dimensions - we each have a cause to defend. The fact that we choose deliberately a route against the existing rules of society shows our scorn of others, our truthfulness to life - to say before everyone that the hypocrisy of the society today is not a very elegant path to take. One cannot merely complain about an existing evil you understand, one must do more than open one´s mouth: one must act, must show the way, give an example to follow ..."

Gary proved faithful to his responsibilities. He was a good father in his own way, but he never quite realised how the anti-conformist decision they had taken was so much easier for him than for Claude. However, Claude never complained of the disparity in their tasks. Maybe she was convinced that things were equal, that they really had shared out the responsibilities equally. Claude did not take part in the social revolutionary movements of 1968, but was an early example of this new spirit, the embodiment of the more vital face of 1960s feminism: the proud assertion that women were independent of men, without rejecting men out of hand, however, and without renouncing one's own femininity.

1963 was an important year for Gary. He was about to become a father and had to find a stable job. When in Scotland he had met a Swede who had a business in Stockholm, and who had offered him a job as ´export manager´. The job involved selling cars in North Africa. North Africa! - travel, adventure - even if the work was boring. And it would be a permanent job that would allow him to send regular payments to Claude for their child. This was a brilliant opportunity to compromise between the necessity for more stability with his intolerance of routine work. Gary wrote to Mr. Gutemberg that he would willingly take the job, and was ready to start as soon as possible. He was informed that he would have to wait a few months, and this struck him as perfect. Why not, before committing himself to a permanent job, try for some great climb.

Together with John he decided to spend the summer months climbing in the Mont Blanc massif. One of the routes planned was a new, aesthetic ascent on the Fou, in the Chamonix Aiguilles. Before travelling north, he trained with his French friends on the lesser mountains around Grenoble.

While in Grenoble, Gary met a Scottish climber, one Stewart Fulton. As he had not friends in the country and spoke very poor French, Gary put him up and took him on climbing trips. They did several ascents in the Vercors and the Chartreuse, and even a couple of new ascents on the Pic de Bure and the Rocher du Midi. Stewart was not the ideal companion for Gary who found his laziness irritating.

He criticised him for not helping to prepare for their climbs, and for not putting enough effort into learning the techniques for using pitons and rope. However, he was a good climber, and Gary invited him onto the project on the Fou.

In June they went to Chamonix and walked up to the Envers des Aiguilles hut. John was already there with Konrad Kirch, the young German who went missing on the Punta Gugliermina two years earlier. He had kept in touch with John and had become his climbing companion. They had even climbed the North Face of the Eiger together! John had been obsessed with this climb and his dream was finally realised. They were both in great shape.

The day before Gary and Stewart arrived, John and Konrad had climbed the couloir that leads to the start of the route, but had encountered problems with the snow and had turned back early for fear of avalanches. They reckoned that the face presented more problems than anticipated. Apparently there was a very large overhang which would be very difficult to get up. And the weather was very poor with the climbing season one month late in coming. Then they did not have enough gear: they needed horizontal pegs, RURPs and bongs, and they had hardly enough normal pegs to use on the overhang if they had to climb with pegs and etriers or needed to abseil down again. On top of all this, a snow storm blew up and so the four could only go back home.

Gary went on to the Calanques. Down there the sun always shines, and Gary relaxed by climbing on the white cliffs which fall vertically into the blue sea.

He returned to Chamonix in July with Claude and

Fulton to find John waiting for them with his wife Mara. Konrad Kirch could not make it this time, but an old friend had arrived. Tom Frost had just got back from Nepal where he had been with Ed Hillary, building schools for Sherpas - and of course they had taken the opportunity to do a few climbs. He had come to Chamonix to spend the summer in the Alps and he joined their group with enthusiasm. Tom had climbed with Robbins on some of the most difficult 'firsts' in Yosemite. He was a good free climber and unbeatable at artificial climbing. Moreover, he was a skilled technician and had brought with him a wide range of chrome-molybdenum pegs produced by Chouinard. These could not be found in Europe, and were essential for their planned ascent, which they expected to be exacting. The pegs were very durable - once removed from a tight crack they would return to their original shape, and could be used many times with complete safety. With Tom was his fiancée, Dorene, who soon became good friends with Claude and Mara.

The ascent of the south face of the Fou really was more difficult than they had expected. At their first attempt they managed to get over the first overhang and to traverse along a diagonal crack. They prepared to bivouac on a very narrow ledge, but John and Stewart's hammock broke and they had to spend the night on a system of rope ladders. Next morning it was raining and all four turned back. The second attempt was no better, despite the first pitches going much faster with the help of the fixed ropes left at the most overhung points. Again it rained and Stewart suffered a hand injury - nothing serious, but they would be better to turn back.

On the evening of July 24th , Tom and Stewart returned to the route with Dorene and bivouacked at its base. The next day, very early, Gary and John, with Claude and Mara, climbed the south-east ridge of the Blaitière, their descent bringing them to the bivouac under the Fou. Dorene and Claude stayed at the bivouac, and Mara returned to the hut with two friends who had helped to carry the material for the third attempt.

The four men started again on the route, quickly climbing up to their previous high point. From there, Tom climbed another overhang by means of what John called an ´engineering masterpiece´, using both minuscule pegs in almost invisible cracks, and a ten centimetre bong. On top of the overhang there was a wide ledge, perfect for a bivouac.

Just as they were settling for the evening, it started to hail and continued to storm all night long. The four climbers were safe enough in their bivouac bags secured to the ledge, but they feared the bolts of lightning which came in rapid succession, strange, dazzling flashes uncomfortably near. The brightness of the lightning also kept the two women awake all night, in their bivouac at the foot of the face. Before settling down for the night, they had climbed a rocky spur opposite the route, and had followed the four climbers' ascent. Having seen them arrive safely on the ledge, they would not have been worried for them had it not been for the lightning. By morning the storm had died down and at first light, John and Gary took turns to lead the rest of the ascent.

They had opened one of the most aesthetic and most difficult routes in the Alps, but once again Gary and John displayed their incompatibility. From start to finish they had discussed and criticised each other's every move, and while descending they had come close to blows. John had accused Gary of dislodging some stones which had just missed him. Gary was furious, particularly as he was always very careful not to loosen any stones, and he moved menacingly towards John. John came to meet him with his fist raised and if Stewart Fulton had not stepped between them things could have turned nasty. In addition, John had publicised their ascent before starting off and when they returned they were met by journalists, photographers and admirers. John was in his element and played the part of the lion.

Gary had been against publicity from the start and refused to take part in such a spectacle. Maybe he was jealous of John's success, who, with his Hollywood-star looks and his easy relations with the public, had assumed the major role; or maybe Gary was beginning to realise that climbing was not that important for him. Whatever the reason, he returned to Grenoble earlier than planned. John and Tom were invited as American representatives to an international climbing congress in Chamonix, and they spent the rest of the summer there, making numerous climbs and opening a new, demanding route on the Hidden Pillar of the Frêney face.

In Grenoble Gary had much to organise before leaving for Sweden. He also wanted to finish the first chapter of his book, which he had promised to send to the director of the magazine La Montagne, and with which he had made good progress.

Then he met a Canadian who told him that in Canada they were looking for French teachers. Gary, who always made the mistake of attributing his own desires and dreams to others, tried to persuade Claude to go to Canada. She would have to hurry because the child was to be born in January. He would visit her from time to time and maybe even find some work there at some point. Or they could travel to Australia. Gary's imagination would often take over and he would dream of his child growing up in Canada or Australia, with their vast, isolated areas, free from the fateful influence of America's imperialistic politics and the threatening presence of the Soviet Union. He did not want his child to live in a Europe which was divided in two and sitting on a ticking bomb. For some time, Gary had been preoccupied with thoughts of nuclear war and he was worried for his child's safety. Claude had absolutely no intention of moving to Canada or Australia: she loved her town, her work and her friends, and was very attached to Europe and its culture. They discussed this subject night and day, and though the talks were endless, they were constructive.

During this period Gary did a lot of thinking. He had then been in Europe for three years and had almost lost sight of the ambitions that brought him here: to gain wider experience and become a writer. Of course he had also come here to climb, but that was not his only aim. He wrote:

" ... all of these goals are like so many small peaks which block the climber's view of the real summit, very high and very far away and upon climbing those smaller peaks he may or may not be able to see the distant summit but whether he can or cannot he still is just as far away, if not farther - since now in order to attain it he must disengage himself from this smaller peak that he has attained and descend from it and try to find a route thru the valleys and ridges below."

Gary wanted to head for the real summit and he set to work patiently on the smaller peaks. His book on California climbing was an ambitious project which comprised history, techniques and the philosophy of climbing in his country. He was in no hurry to complete his work, but wanted rather to achieve perfection. He put a lot of work into the first chapter concerning the principles of climbing in general. Claude helped him with his French, correcting his drafts, but had also helped by discussing the various issues with him. Gary wanted to add her name to his work, and the first chapter was published in the form of an article in the magazine La Montagne, with both their signatures and titled ´A la recherche d'un équilibre´. This was a very important article for the world of alpinism as it put into words the philosophy of the new generation of those times. Gary had spent his youth with the Sierra Club, more a nature conservation association than a climbing club, and in this article he talked of the need to protect the environment and nature, subjects which were unknown in 1960s Europe. He also talked of climbing as a personal experience which anyone had the right to enjoy as a form of adventure. He asked climbers to leave as few traces as possible so that those who came after could derive as much pleasure from the discovery of new ground. For the same reasons, he advised against giving overly detailed descriptions of new routes: let others enjoy the delight of finding things out for themselves. And he wrote of the importance of climbing with respect for ethics and the aesthetic nature of the route, without which climbing was degraded to a coarse and senseless series of actions.

By this point in his life, Gary was satisfied with his climbing achievements. He had opened up new and highly acclaimed routes, and had striven to assert himself as a great climber. Having reached this stage, he refused to consider himself as a climber, and even if he continued to climb, he would no longer attribute much importance to his achievements, which he would not even write down any more. He was now moving towards his true goal, the real summit.

CHAPTER TWELVE

From Stockholm to Marrakech

"When I was eight I wanted to climb my first mountain. It was called Black Mountain and was just opposite where I lived in Southern California. It wasn't a real mountain, barely 1,000 metres. I thought about it day and night. Every Sunday I'd set off, but never got to the top. I was too small and it was too difficult.. I finally climbed it when I was 14. But when I got to the summit, it wasn't high enough! And since then, each time I climb a mountain the same thing happens, they're never big enough ...

"The mountain is an initiation, in the real sense of the word. Its a way of putting yourself to test.

"The Indians have a rite which fascinated me as a boy, and still does. When you reach nine or ten years, you have to leave the tribe and live for one week completely alone. And you have to hide because the other men in the tribe have to come looking for you and will kill you if they find you. And when you have passed this test, you have the right to be called a warrior.

"The mountain is an initiation which is renewed every year. You go there, you test yourself, you find yourself again. Afterwards, you are more able to accept yourself.

"You see, I live in the kingdom of dreams: the mountains transport me to the kingdom of reality. Faced with life and death, you test your own sincerity." [12]

The mountains were an initiation for Gary. He had got through the test and earned the right to go out into the world. At a mundane level he still had a few details to arrange with Gutemberg, but everything was in order in Grenoble; Claude was, as usual, self-sufficient and Gary was not worried about her. What did worry him though was the world-wide political situation. Gary grew more and more convinced of the imminence of a nuclear war, and repeatedly tried to persuade Claude to move to Canada, or even better Australia. The death of Kennedy upset him deeply. Gary was convinced that his murder was the result of some conspiracy, even before hints of such appeared in the newspapers. He spent his last days with Claude discussing politics and philosophy, and enjoying their mutual affection.

Finally it was time for him to leave. The date was December 20th 1962. It was only a few days to Christmas, Claude would be alone in Grenoble and the baby could arrive at any time. For the first time, Claude did not manage to hide her emotions and their parting was morose.

Gary left Grenoble hitch-hiking, with a lump in his throat and Christmas presents in his suitcase for Johnny and Andrea, John's children. John had by this time left the Air Force, but not wanting to leave Europe and the Alps. Mara and he had found work with the American School of Leysin in Switzerland, and the family had recently moved there. Gary visited them before travelling north.

Geneva, Lausanne, Basle. Within one and a half days, he was in Copenhagen. His excitement about travelling

[12]   From an interview with Gary Hemming: A. Michel, J-P Clébert, *Légendes et traditions de France*, Paris 1979.

made him forget his sorrow. "The beautiful city of Copenhagen! It is a beauty, no question, and the girls are what they are cracked up to be, marvellous ... " He decided to stop a few days, and wandered around the streets, imagining: "A new book to write: A Climber's Guide to the High Cities ... For any self-respecting good climber the mountain areas require much less guiding info than other areas in this earth - in particular the savage, cruel, big cities."

He met a beautiful girl in some bar and fell in love for a few hours. But after several days, as often with Gary, his enthusiasm turned into intolerance: "Four nights bivouac in Copenhagen - that's far too many. I really couldn't have chosen a more horrible place to spend Christmas ..." He thought of Claude, of their child soon to be born. He could have left after Christmas: his meeting in Sweden was arranged for the first days of January. But he had been afraid that the Christmas atmosphere and the premature birth of his child may have moved him and made him change his plans. Only then did he realise that he had literally run away, escaped.

There was no choice but to go on. In Stockholm he went to meet his new employer. Mr. Gutemberg was a very old man, suffering from diabetes and going blind. He had a son who should have been taking care of business in North Africa, but he had broken a leg and could not travel. That was why Mr. Gutemberg had offered Gary this job. Gary had already sold second-hand cars, and that was what he had to do in Marrakech. Gary would be given a Volkswagen van in which he could live, and once he had arrived in Marrakech, he would receive necessary instructions. Everything seemed rather vague, but the job was supposed to pay well, and this was what interested Gary. He counted on working hard now so that he would not have to work again for the next ten years "even with a couple of wives and three or four children".

Preparations take some time. Gary enjoyed the New Year celebrations in Stockholm which included a pretend battle between the citizens and the police, but he soon grew tired of the city. He hated Stockholm: "The women are too beautiful, the men too well-dressed. Everything is too mechanical and senseless. What a bore. It's like Huxley's New World."

He wrote to Lil, the girl he had met in Copenhagen. "Stockholm is an awful city ... What a great time I had in Copenhagen ...". Poor Gary, constantly disappointed in what he found, always longing for the past and always quick to get excited about anything new, which would only disappoint him soon. He was to spend all his life like this, moving from rushes of excitement to bitter distaste, without ever losing his ability to find enthusiasm for new countries, new women who returned his mischievous smile, a new mountain to climb.

Mr. Gutemberg paid him part of his salary in advance for living costs, and Gary was then able to pay off some small debts and send a cheque to Claude, who would need the money when the baby was born.

They had not yet decided on a name; Claude was to choose one and just ask for his approval. When the baby was born, a boy, Claude decided to call him Sören, after their best-loved philosopher, Sören Kirkegaard. He had been the subject of many of their animated debates, when they had lived together happily. She sent a telegram to Gary "SOREN ERIC EST NE": Sören Eric is born. However, the telegram was misspelt in the Stockholm office, and Gary received the cryptic message: "LOREN ERIC SYNE". Gary replied by telegram, giving his OK to the strange name, Loren Eric Syné. But when Claude went to register the name, she changed it for the French, Lauren.

And so there now was a Lauren Hemming and Gary could not wait to see him. At last the van was ready and he could leave. However, his impatience to see his son did not stop him from travelling via Paris to gaze up at Marie's window. She would not come out, and Gary began to argue with her parents, so possessive, so middle-class ...

The van was a wreck - everything was worn-out: the battery, the oil pump, the alternator. At numerous points in his journey, Gary had to stop for repairs, and it took two weeks to reach Grenoble. Once there he had little time, but Claude was very weak - neither of them had guessed that even a strong woman such as Claude may need some rest after giving birth. She had no one to help her and was depressed, breaking frequently into tears, so Gary postponed his departure a few days.

He left again at the start of February. Near Marseilles he stopped at Calanques to spend the night in the Refuge du Piolet, at the Calanque d'En Vau, where he had been many times with Claude: "Back once more to my most beloved of spots in Europe".

His journey continued. He crossed to Spain and was very attracted to Barcelona, "so perfectly balanced between sea and mountain". Then he took the ferry from Algeciras and reached Africa. Gary was very excited. Within two days he arrived in Marrakech, where he parked the van in the city's campsite and awaited instructions which were to arrive by post.

No news arrived from Gutemberg. Instead he received many letters from Claude, who wrote about the baby and told of what was happening in the Alps. John was not satisfied with having climbed the north face of the Eiger; now he wanted to open a new direttissimo route on the face. And to make this even more spectacular, he wanted to open it in winter. He had already made one attempt with two very talented Italians, Ignazio Piussi and Roberto Sorgato, but they had had to retreat.

The Alps seemed very distant to Gary, stuck in some dusty campsite in an African city. He spent his time writing to Claude, to Marie, to his friends. The days went by and nothing happened.

Eventually he decided that rather than sitting around waiting, he could see a bit of this new country. He liked the city and was attracted by its citizens whom he found beautiful with their regal costumes. The men were so proud and the women so mysterious - and what women, with their eyes flashing above the veil: they were more fascinating than he could have ever imagined. The only problem was that, of all the places he had visited till then, he could not communicate with the people there. Most probably the men distrusted this tall, lanky, blonde figure, and they disliked the way he looked at the women.

Gary travelled south towards the desert, through the Draa valley, Ouazarzate ... " All deserts are alike; only the people are different". He missed the deserts in California. In fact he missed California, he missed Wyoming; he missed France, the Alps. He wanted to go back, go climbing again, maybe an even more direct route on the west face of the Dru [13], to climb the Linceul [The Shroud], a vertical ice wall on the north face of the Grandes Jorasses ... He wrote to Chouinard to involve him in these projects, but without the enthusiasm and conviction of the previous year.

If only Claude were with him ... Or Marie ...

He travelled north again towards the Atlas: "an area which resembles the mountainous deserts of California and Nevada". He slept out under the stars: "If Claude was here she would really like this place. And she would be able to get on with the people".

He wanted to climb Toubkal, the highest summit in the Atlas, towering over 4,000 metres. But at such altitudes in winter there would be a lot of snow, even in Africa, and Gary did not have strong enough boots or warm clothes to protect him from the chilling wind.

So he returned to Marrakech and finally found a letter from Gutemberg at the Post Office; but the instructions were vague, dubious. Gary grew suspicious of the whole business and successive instructions justified his doubts - the infamous cars were to be sold on the black market. Gary gave much thought to the decision between carrying on and packing it all in. He needed money: he had a son now, he could not live just day to day. But Mr. Gutemberg made the decision for him, suddenly all communications stopped - he had disappeared.

Gary still did not know what to do. He had met a young German couple who had been at the campsite for a

---

[13] Opened by Harlin and Robbins the following year.

few weeks. He was attracted to the girl who reminded him of his mother and of Mara Harlin. Naturally Klaus did not appreciate Gary's attitude towards his fiancee, and their friendship came to an abrupt end. For Gary, the campsite was already unpleasant, but now that he was at odds with those living near him, he could no longer bear it. To make things worse, Gary had argued with a Frenchman in the Post Office, who had addressed him in the familiar form in French, and had insulted him when Gary had pointed out that he was not his brother. Gary had tried to hit the man, but had received a punch in the mouth before he could touch his opponent. This always happened to him when he got into a fight. And as if a cut lip was not enough, the police arrived and Gary had a moment of real panic when he thought of the letters in his pocket from Gutemberg, giving details of the illegal sale of the cars.

Enough was enough, he had to leave. He would sell the van and buy a plane ticket for France, but it was not that easy to find a buyer. When he had first arrived, at least ten Moroccans had approached him and asked him to sell the van. But now that it came to getting out their money, no one wanted to know. And so these Arabs, so colourful, so "proud and mysterious" seemed to him miserable beggars and they disgusted him. By then Gary had really had enough of the dirty, almost deserted campsite, and he had even got lice.

By a stroke of luck, he met Joseph, an old Frenchman and ex-alpinist, who lived in Casablanca and who invited Gary to stay in his house. In Casablanca, Gary's good mood and good luck returned. He managed to sell the van and bought a ticket to Paris.

CHAPTER THIRTEEN

Back to America

In Paris, Gary finally managed to arrange a meeting with Marie. By that time she had got engaged, but this did not prevent her from flirting with Gary - just enough to rekindle his passion, but refusing him when he asked her to leave for the States with him. Only then did Gary realise that he did not love "the Marie of flesh and blood, but the image of Marie, of a young, gracious but rebellious girl". For the first time, he was able to see Marie with disenchantment, but this moment of realisation was short-lived. Deep down, Marie did not want to lose Gary, and she won him over with promises that she would think of him, she would leave her fiance and her family, and leave with him.

In a rush of renewed love and faith, Gary gave those of his diaries that he had with him to Marie, and promised that she could also read his future writings. From that moment on, Gary introduced a subconscious censorship to his diaries, adapting them for Marie's eyes. Marie would then return these to him, having added her comments, often of a trite nature, but which Gary would consider as profound observations. Gary stayed in Paris until Marie left for Tunisia on holiday with her parents. Only then did he return to Grenoble.

There he found Claude in tears because he had spent so much time with ´her´, before coming to see them. For so long now Claude had been strong. She knew about Marie, had never complained, and Gary should have understood and excused her for being upset about having to wait around for him. But no! The tiniest breach of their ´pact´ and he exploded and unjustly turned on her: she wanted to appear progressive, have an open mind, but instead she was only a "possessive bourgeois. She is not brave, she can't live alone. She doesn't realise that for two years I have been trying to get the only person I love and have each time been defeated". Gary could not see his own selfishness. However, after only a few days, anger was replaced by the old harmony in their relationship. Gary felt ashamed of his behaviour, and through his diaries, examined his conscience: "I got angry with her only because I was annoyed by feeling trapped by my responsibilities. As soon as Claude starts to think of our relationship as an adventure again, I fall back in love with her. She is the bravest woman I know, together with my mother." He felt embarrassed also because he had hid certain important details from Claude. She did not know that he had asked Marie to go the States with him, and he had not told her that he had given his diaries to Marie, when he had not even let Claude look at them. He really had been unfair, but unfortunately, "as with life, there is no justice in love".

They spent that summer together in Chamonix, camping in the usual campsite. They went for long walks together, and one day climbed up to the Refuge d'Argentière. But Gary's vision of the mountains had changed from the previous years: " I'm surrounded here by huge walls of ice and snow like seldom is ever seen. Huge hopeless walls with no pity. Austere, aloof from mortal beings. How can one dare to climb such things as these? These are real men's walls. To engage oneself on such walls as these is to engage all one's life. These are walls of life or death for those who would climb them."

While he was writing in his diary, Claude sat a few metres from him. "Going back to the mountains has made her beautiful again. No other woman is as beautiful as her in the mountains." Only when he was near her did Gary achieve tranquillity.

After a few days, Claude went back to Grenoble, and Gary wrote more and more letters to Marie in Tunisia. He wanted to convince her to travel to Montreal where he would meet her and they would go on together to the States. By then he had decided to go back to the States and had already written to all his friends and girlfriends, even to Judith, notifying them. Marie replied to his letters, but would not make up her mind to leave. Gary bought her a plane ticket from Tunisia to Montreal; it was not used.

So Gary stayed on a while in Chamonix. He was waiting for John who had plans on the Dru - the famous direttissima on the west face. John arrived accompanied by Pierre Mazeaud and Alec Kunaver, a Yugoslav alpinist he had included in his attempts on the ´super direct´ on the Eiger.

Gary and John, on meeting again, got involved in a rather violent discussion. John had thought of completing the route using siege tactics: climbing it in pitches and descending every day to climb back up again the next day on fixed ropes, then moving on to the next pitch, until the summit was reached. Gary did not agree with this tactic. The previous year he had been unhappy with the route on the Fou, which had been climbed partly using this method, even if this was not deliberate - poor weather having forced them to descend. There seemed no solution to their disagreement, so Gary left the group.

It is not known whether Gary did any other climbs that season in Chamonix. It is improbable that he stayed all that time at the foot of the Mont Blanc massif without climbing, but there is no mention of routes in his diary, and he did not talk of any climbs to his friends. However, he did leave Chamonix long before the season was over, and returned to Grenoble. He entrusted a trunk to Claude - locked! - and asked her to send some climbing gear to Jackson.

His farewell with Claude was an emotional one. Gary felt a rekindling of his passion for her.

By the 20th July, Gary was in New Jersey, staying with Sterling Neale.

The next stage of his journey took him to New York, where he met Judith again. After all, she had been a great love of his, and he had often thought of her and had written several times from France. Outwardly, she still looked the same, but after less than an hour, Gary was already annoyed about having come to see her. "You need a shave, comb your hair,

your hair is too long, why don't you get your teeth fixed ... ".
My God! how did he ever put up with her?

Too much time had passed. America seemed so
different from the country he had left behind. On the streets,
on the subway, there was a tense, brutal atmosphere that
he had never noticed before. One evening in a bar in Rhode
Island, he took a good look at the people around him. They
were strangers, they did not know each other, they did not
have anything against each other, but, he later wrote to a
friend, "the violence and hate that was there was so thick I
could cut it with a knife".

Hitch-hiking back from Rhode Island to New York,
two young men stopped in a new, flashy limousine, but
after driving some distance, they ran out of petrol and the
car stopped at the roadside. Two policemen stopped and
approached the car, and suddenly, the two boys jumped
out of the car and ran off into the woods. Gary sat in the
car, stupefied, not understanding what was going on. It
turned out that the car was stolen, and Gary was retained
for questioning. However, they treated him with respect
and called him Mister Hemming. Here things were more
friendly than in the pub in Rhode Island. With relief Gary
could at last recognise the real America, the America he
had always carried in his heart, the America of the
Declaration of Independence, the civilised America where
each citizen is sacred and everyone was innocent until
proved guilty.

But ... they came to wake him in the middle of the
night in his cell. Once again, his diaries had got him into
trouble. The policemen had read them, and now accused
Gary of obscenity. Gary's use of profane language had

actually become relatively chaste since Marie had started reading his diaries, but it was still vulgar enough to shock the police. To make matters worse there was a photograph of Claude, breast feeding Lauren. Suddenly Gary was no longer Mister Citizen, but Mister Suspect, and the faces around him were harsh, as had been the faces in the Rhode Island pub.

Eventually they let him go, with the advice that he should get a haircut.

Before travelling west, Gary stopped off in the 'Gunks. He had few friends there and did not find any familiar faces; but some new acquaintances let him try out mescalin. This was the first time he had ever taken any form of drugs. From time to time, Marie had secretly smoked marijuana - one of the reasons Gary regarded her as such a rebel! Gary disapproved of the use of these substances, and often lectured her about this, only provoking sulks and arguments. But mescalin, with the feeling induced of widening one's awareness, was a revelation for Gary.

The next stage of his journey was to Jackson, and the first thing Gary did on arriving was to go to the Post Office to pick up Claude's letters. His climbing gear had also arrived. Then he met his old friends again. They were all there - Barry Corbet, Bill Briggs, Pete Sinclair, Mort Hempel ... Even Royal Robbins was there with his wife. Gary was glad to be back in the Tetons, but being back among his friends did not make him as happy as he had expected. They all seemed different to him, middle class, weakened by the comforts of material things. In truth, some of them had got married, had begun to concentrate on work ... The carelessness of youth cannot last for ever.

He joined one of the infamous 'Teton Tea Parties', just like in the old times, but soon left the group to sit alone on the banks of Jenny Lake, to go on a 'trip' with mescalin. In his induced state of lucidity, he reflected on how he had wandered through life heading towards false targets - University, climbing, adventures - and came to the conclusion that his life had been one big escape, while searching for something he had never found. Maybe travelling the world over had been a mistake; maybe what he was looking for had been right there at home, right beside him, and he had not been able to see it ....

Maybe the mescalin helped him to find what he wanted, or maybe the influence of these places really was very strong; whatever the case, Gary decided to stay in Jackson, to find some form of stability.

He wrote to Claude: "I've managed to find a job working in the woods cutting trees that is hard and healthy and pays well and every nite I come back to the campground here at Jenny Lake tired and hungry, but it is a good tired feeling, and I've taken up with a young girl here (whose husband has left her stranded here in Wyoming with a two year old kid and a tent while he left in a huff back to NY) so I have even the semblance of family life for as long as it pleases the two of us."

And he enjoyed his work - he liked getting up early and walking for an hour or two before reaching the trees to be cut. He grew drunk on the smell of the resin mixed with the bracing fresh air found at 3,000 metres. He did not tire of the physical fatigue, but felt good, healthy and strong. The countryside was beautiful, its colours exquisite.

The summer went by without Gary getting tired of this lifestyle, and it seemed that his eternal restlessness had left him. He wrote often to Claude, telling of his life with Peggy. They had rented a small apartment in the town of Jackson, not being able to live in a tent with a two-year-old child. This was not meant to be a permanent arrangement, partly because unmarried couples living together was still considered improper in the States - despite the fact that they cared little for general opinion, they felt uneasy. Things would be different in Europe! "and of course my work is great. Peggy is teaching me to paint". But this apparent idyll was disturbed by a feeling of apprehension that he could not shake off: "I fear this place. I am afraid of this country. There is such violence in the air. This whole country is Goldwater. Here in Wyoming 9 out of 10 will vote for him in November."

Wyoming is a conservative area, one of the last 'border' areas. There are a few ranches spread out over vast areas, cattle have kilometres upon kilometres of grazing land and cowboys roam the open land for weeks. When they get back to town they head straight for the saloon even before taking off their leather breeches, and drink themselves stupid. "How could such people have progressive thoughts, or even democratic ideas?"

One evening in a saloon, Gary began to argue with a certain cowboy called Evans. For some time they had been exchanging scowls - Gary did not like Evans, in fact he hated him because he "embodied everything I hate about the States". And naturally the cowboy did not like Gary because he felt Gary's scorn. Gary never could learn to keep his mouth shut, and that evening he went too far. Evans

left the saloon without a word, and when Gary eventually
left, three cowboys followed him and cornered him in an
alley. They had clubs and Gary could not defend himself.
They left him lying on the ground, much the worse for wear,
his left leg fractured, a broken jaw and cuts all over his
body.

Someone had warned Peggy, who came running,
frightened out of her mind. She found him lying there,
unconscious. She dragged him to her car and drove him to
the hospital. Gary was badly disfigured, but when he wrote
to Claude he tried to minimise the seriousness of his
injuries, joking:

"At the moment the doctors have my upper jaw
wired to my lower to keep it from falling off. My right eye
is glued on with some new type of surgical tape and is not
bad except that it keeps looking up in the sky all the time.
I don't have a left ear anymore. They tell me it's been eaten
by a spectator."

When he was finally discharged from hospital, on crutches,
he could no longer bear to stay. He was sorry to leave Peggy,
but he could not take one day more: "I escape from violence.
I'll never come back to that valley again. This time I'm
determined never to come back to the States, once I leave.
It's a question of SURVIVAL. Death is chasing me in this
country. I have to leave before it catches me."

Before leaving Jackson - no one knows why - he went
to the cemetery. This was in an isolated spot, halfway up a
hill over the town, facing the mountains. He wandered for
some time among the graves, looking at each one. In his
diary, he wrote: "From here the Grand Teton is visible and

Mount Owen and Teewinot as well. But the colours are brown, green and yellow, dull not brilliant. It's higher up where the reds and violets and shining greens are to be found. From here Jackson could be a desert village - an oasis as much as a wild west mountain town. And that sun so warm - that breeze so warm ... "

PART TWO

CHAPTER FOURTEEN

A Patchwork of Assorted Truths

I visited the cemetery in Jackson Hole, one bright March morning. The sun was warm, so warm ... But the gravestones were covered in a metre of snow. I asked Bill Briggs, who came with me, to show me Gary's grave, but Bill could not . He had never been to the graveyard before that day.

"Who can tell me which one it is?"

"His mother. His mother was the only one who went to the funeral."

Bill's house is about five minutes from the cemetery, outside Jackson and near the Snow King ski complex, with ski lifts, hotel with indoor swimming pool, sauna and Jacuzzi. Bill is at home at Snow King. He worked on the design of the slopes and manages the ski school. "Hi Bill!" "Hello Bill!". Everyone treats him with the friendly respect granted to the local legends of every town. Some fifteen years ago, Bill skied down the sheer east face of the Grand

Teton - legendary in itself.

Bill came with me to Jenny Lake. We had to go some distance on skis because the road was still blocked by snow. Even the lake was frozen and covered in snow; its shape barely visible in the vast stretch of ground after the last trees. It is a beautiful area in winter, completely isolated, and smelling freshly of pine. It must be even more marvellous in summer, with the blue lake, the green grass and colourful flowers ... Gary loved this place more than any other. Together with the Calanques. He would say: the two most beautiful places in the world are the Tetons and the Calanques.

Bill stopped:

"Just there, where your skis are - that's where I found Gary's body."

One month later I was visiting Pierre Joffroy in Paris.

"I've finished. I went back to the States, and this time I met almost all of them. I spent two days with his mother. She didn't tell me anything about him, only things about her family. But even her reticence is important, to be able to understand. I've been to Jackson Hole. I've talked to everyone who was there when he died. Almost everyone. Their stories coincide, at least for the important details."

"And what conclusions have you reached?"

"Do you mean about the murder theory? No, it doesn't bear close examination. I think that that story came about because so many people knew Gary as being full of life, ideas, energy, and they couldn't accept the thought of his suicide."

"And you, what do you think, now that you've talked

with so many people who knew him, and that you've made your own impression of him?"

"I've my own theory, naturally, but I'm not sure whether it's right for a biographer to write with some theory in mind. It could ruin my claim to objectivity."

"On the contrary. It would be bad news if a biographer did not have some personal ideas about the characters and events. So what is your theory?"

"I don't believe it was murder, and it's not so improbable that Gary shot himself. His moods changed and he went from extreme lows to highs, lost his temper and could get quite depressed... There had been a quarrel that afternoon, in the campsite near Jenny Lake. Everyone had drunk a lot. Gary more than the others, maybe, and alcohol was bad for him: throughout the stories I've heard, Gary always seemed to be violent when he had been drinking. And so once again, he had tried to start a fight, provoking people. At one point he challenged Mike Lowe to a fight. In his defence, it has to be said that he chose someone bigger than himself. Mike is six foot two inches, and sturdy, not thin like Gary, and everyone knew that Mike was a judo expert. It didn't take him long to floor Gary, not to hurt him, but to keep him under control, because the state he was in he could have hurt someone."

"And then?"

"Then Bill Briggs arrived, led him away and talked to him for some time to try to calm him down. When he left him, Gary was calm and went off to find Muffy by the car."

"And did he stay with Muffy?"

"No. He got his rucksack, and his gun he kept in the

sack - he even fired a shot into the air - but then he went off. And that was the last thing that happened before the second shot was fired."

"So no one was with him when the second shot was fired."

"No".

"And where was everyone?"

"Well, they'd all gone to sleep: some in tents; others in houses - at that time there were some log cabins beside the lake - and some slept in their cars. Bill Briggs was in his van when he heard the shot."

"And nobody went to see what had happened?"

"But nobody thought something serious had happened. In America, it's quite common to carry a gun, and fire it for fun - just like in the films, especially in that cowboy land - and so gun shot is not as alarming for them as it would be for us. And those who saw the fight thought that Gary was off in the woods, walking off his drunkenness and firing shots all over the place, so they thought it best not to go outside in case they got shot by mistake. And if you think about it - who would want to go out in the woods in the middle of the night when some drunk fool was wandering around with a gun in his hand? It doesn't seem so strange to me ... And anyway, all the stories coincide. No one was with Gary when the second shot was fired."

"What I find strange is that these accounts still coincide after twenty years. You forget things with time, your memories change ... And the theories of suicide were doubted from the very start. What if there was some plot? I don't mean that Gary's murder was planned, but maybe there was an accident, during the fight a shot was fired ...

Someone tried to get the gun out of Gary's hand and fired it by mistake when it was pointed at Gary. It would seem probable that all those there would agree to help the unwitting murderer and would have made up a story for the police which they agreed to keep secret all their life. This would explain why their stories fit so well."

"It's not impossible, but not so probable. It seems that during the fight with Mike, Gary didn't have the gun. And anyway, the ´clinical´ image of Gary's personality points to the possibility of suicide. Why reject the most simple theory, and also the one already accepted?"

"Because it's so strange that Gary should commit suicide. He had gone to Alaska to earn some money so he could join Françoise and marry her. He had plans: how could anyone with such happy plans kill themselves?"

"But I've found out that his dreams of happiness were falling to pieces. Françoise had met someone else in Nairobi. Gary was unhappy, he wrote to her every day and was waiting for her reply but it never arrived ... So you see, you cannot rule out depression."

"That's too simple and I'm not convinced. Gary was not the type to give up so easily. No, you have to get to the bottom of the investigations, start all over again if necessary ... "

Even I was not convinced by the simpler explanations. If we are to believe that Gary's death was voluntary, we have to know what provoked him to take his own life.

It was at that point that Pierre Joffroy allowed me to read Gary's diaries.

He had kept me waiting for years, but all the time helping me with titbits of information. When I met him for the first time - I got his address from René Desmaison - he was very diffident. He wanted to know why I had decided to write about Gary's life, wanted to know in full the information I had already gathered. This was little. I had begun my research by writing to those people whose names appeared in climbing journals beside Gary's. Ken Wilson, English alpinist and journalist and founder of *Mountain* magazine, encouraged me and provided me with some addresses. Then I had been in Chamonix to look through the local newspaper files and to talk to people who may have known Gary.

"You have to go to America," Joffroy told me, "you have to meet his mother, his friends from school. You have to find out his date of birth, what he studied, where he did his military service. He said that he had been a cadet in the Air Force Academy in Denver and had been expelled, but that could be a tall story - he liked to tell fibs from time to time."

Joffroy gave me some old addresses, but most of my letters were returned: addressee unknown or moved. So I went for the first time to America, and spoke to some of Gary's friends, spread over many cities, most with different time zones. I gathered some new addresses, wrote to other people, and returned to visit Joffroy. He was satisfied with the new work I presented to him, and told me about the diaries. Gary had left him a trunk with all he owned in it, before leaving on his last journey to the States. With the trunk he had written a note in large letters: "In the event of an accident, burn everything". Fortunately Pierre Joffroy went against his instructions.

"The diaries belong to Gary's son. You have to visit him and ask for his permission to read them."

He also gave me several other old addresses, but they all seemed to be outdated. Then, one day, a letter arrived from Claude. In principle she was not opposed to a biography, but she was perturbed. "The life of a person who is no longer with us no longer concerns just the person himself, but all those he involved in his life and who have survived him. The biographer has to respect the living, has to be discreet." But how can a biographer promise discretion? A biography is in itself a violation of private lives which no delicate language can hide. And there is no sense in writing a reticent biography - it is of no use, and would lack interest. I could not promise the discretion Claude requested, but I could convince her of my good intentions, and of my seriousness. She accepted my arguments.

I went back to Pierre Joffroy with the permission from Gary's son to read the diaries, but he said that this was not the right time:

"You have not met his mother yet," he told me, "and you have to go to Jackson Hole to try to gain some insight into Gary's death."

Some people had already told me about that night by Jenny Lake, and I had received a long letter from Bill Briggs containing all the details. I had also visited Barry Corbet, who had provided me with some particularly enlightening details. I really did not want to go back to the States, but Pierre Joffroy insisted:

"How can you write the biography of a person

without having seen the places where he lived, and the place where he died?"

At that point, I thought of giving up, but then I received a letter from Barry Corbet. "When I saw you, there was something I didn't tell you, something my subconscious kept hidden even from me. Somewhere in the back of my mind, was the memory of Gary's rucksack which he left with me in Denver, before leaving for the Tetons. I went to go and find it. Do you want to know what was in it?". He listed its contents in his letter: among letters and various objects, there were a gun, a Bible and an American flag about the size of a handkerchief.

Claude had given me Gary's mother's new address, and I left on my second journey to the States.

And so, I had completed all the tests, and Pierre Joffroy handed the diaries over to me. I panicked when I first opened the trunk in the cellar - there were at least forty notebooks, all numbered, every page covered in small handwriting.

Joffroy told me, "At least twenty diaries are missing. After Gary's death, I met all the three 'widows' to decide what to do with the diaries. Marie took those which concerned her most, and didn't want to give them back."

Reading the diaries proved an extremely embarrassing experience. It had not been easy interviewing people who had been close to Gary, with the sole purpose of wrenching from them their innermost emotions; but reading his diaries was far worse, a pure act of voyeurism. But necessary.

Only then did I realise how wise Pierre Joffroy had

been in not handing over the diaries before I had completed my research. If I had received them earlier, probably I would not have considered it necessary to continue other forms of research, and would have formed an incomplete, one-sided picture of Gary's personality. The image of Gary you get from his diaries is that which Gary had of himself - far different from that I had gathered from talking with people who had known him. And these two images were so contradictory that I found it extremely difficult to accept them at the same time. When I finally succeeded in finding connections between the facts and the judgements, I realised that all these different parts were the pieces of a jigsaw I was trying to complete, even though some pieces had to lie on top of others, and even though I felt that I should discard several pieces. When I had completed my patchwork puzzle, I was able to see that the superfluous and contradictory pieces were all truths, assorted maybe, but still truths.

CHAPTER FIFTEEN

A Hero of the Sixties

"He had many qualities and a magnetic personality. But what did he make of his qualities, and what good did they do for himself and those close to him?" Tom Frost asked this desolate question.

Tom Frost is a profoundly religious man, and religion abhors suicide. It is painful when someone we love dies, but it must be unbearable to know that that someone has taken their own life.

Other religious people who had a high regard for Gary refused to believe in his suicide, mainly because they did not want to accept that he had done something so completely negative. In general, news of his suicide, rather than evoking feelings of compassion, stirred up emotions of rejection and consternation.

Royal Robbins wrote an obituary for Gary, which was published in an American magazine: "Gary's death, because of his vitality, is peculiarly shocking. One feels even a bit angry, for in taking his life, he has taken something from us too. It is surely a high form of credit to a man that his friends feel no pity, but cheated and angry that he is gone." [14]

What did Gary make of his qualities? What good did he do for himself and those close to him? Despite the love and great admiration Gary inspired in people, the story of his life sketches out a far from exemplary personality, full of contradictions, with generous intentions but often selfish actions. His relationship with his son and Claude, for example, was hardly an altruistic one. It is true that Claude and he had both agreed to the open nature of their relationship, but Gary's manner of always running off to follow his impossible and short-lived love stories, and his superficial treatment of those closest to him, did not make him a model partner. But Gary was fond of his son. Not only did he make sure his monthly maintenance payments arrived - a rule certainly sacred, but such payments were difficult to come by for someone like Gary, wandering from small job to small job - but he was also proud of his son, and loved him in his own way, as he loved Claude. Claude's problem was that she was always there for him, whenever he turned up. If Claude had not been so devoted and had made Gary believe that he might lose her, maybe Gary might have taken more care of her. There was one time Claude fell ill, while Gary was in Morocco, and she did not write to him for a few weeks. Gary was desperate - he wrote to all his friends in Grenoble and Chambery to ask them to visit her and see what was going on. However, Claude was too proud to revert to such tricks, and too honest for such thoughts even to enter her mind. And besides, they may not have worked. Maybe Claude, in her role as mother to

[14] Issue no. 6 (November 1969) of *Mountain* magazine, the same obituary signed by Royal Robbins was published, with a slight modification at the end: "Hemming was a man of intense vitality, and this makes his death particularly shocking. One even feels a bit angry, for,

Gary's baby, would not have been able to assume the position of the ideal woman for Gary (the impossible love), and it is quite possible that if Claude had tried to play tricks with Gary's feelings, he would have felt betrayed and would have come to hate her.

However, Gary's restlessness is insufficient explanation for his actions. He was possessed with a fear of being trapped, which can most probably be traced back to his childhood. This was spent in an entirely female environment - his mother, grandmother, aunt/sister, and no male company. His mother did remarry after some years, and Gary's relationship with his stepfather appeared to have been good, but possibly by that time, the seeds of Gary's future love-fear relationship with women were sown.

Even so, his fear of women, or of a commitment to one woman, does not explain Gary's behaviour, and it is impossible to understand his actions except in the context of his times. Gary did not take part in the student marches in Berkeley (he went to the University of California in Berkeley, in 1956 and 57, but left for Europe in 1960), and he missed out on the student riots in Paris in May 1968 (when he was in Sweden with Françoise). But Gary was a real son of the sixties and he avidly followed all the events.

Gary was American to his very soul and he held to the great traditions of American democracy with a kind of religious fervour. He would give lengthy lectures to his French friends on the superiority of Jefferson´s Declaration of Independence over any other constitutional charter from other countries. The right to ´pursuit of happiness´

in taking his own life, he has taken something from us too. Here was a man who would go all the way, one of those whose volcanic energy expands the awareness and enriches the lives of all around them. A lone, lonely, courageous, unique American mountaineer who will not be replaced."

guaranteed in the American Constitution, he would maintain, was the most liberal and most humane principle of all time. Gary did not approve of American politics however, and was particularly critical of imperialism and the Vietnam war. He declared that he was a ´citizen of the world´, but was proud to be an American and loved his country. This was evident from the American flag which he carried in his rucksack wherever he went.

During those years, the seeds of this liberal movement were growing in America, and would soon develop in Europe. Gary's arrival in France coincided with the start of this radical attitude.

The disputes which came to a head in 1968 were directed towards authority, conventional respectability and the bureaucratic institutions which Gary detested most. He lived through (and with) the disputes, but did not take part in the Movement itself. He was, in fact, a precursor of certain sixties fashions. This was mainly the reason behind his popularity when he was thrown before the public eye after the rescue on the Dru. His appearance was tailor-made to attract attention and sympathy at that time: long hair, red jumper, old, dirty jeans and scarf trailing along the ground. He was the perfect image to represent protest, and his reputation as an alpinist-poet-hippie provided a remarkable support for his image.

Gary's sudden and excessive fame can then only be explained against the background of the collective images of those times. During the second half of the 1960s, two posters were sold in their millions all over the world: the famous poster of Bob Dylan designed by Milton Glaser, and that of Che Guevara photographed by Alberto Korda. Likewise, in order to understand Gary's behaviour, you have to look to the disputes and opinions of those times, which publicly challenged the governmental institutions (school, army, even Parliament), and privately changed family life, the life of a couple and the individual roles of partners.

There has never been a revolution which has not contested that nucleus of society - the couple. Even before Engels wrote of the family as the origin of all institutional authoritarianism, revolutionists of all ages anticipated his words. 'Free love' has always played an important part in every new subversive movement against society. However, Hemming probably had not read Engels [15], being too American to read one of the two major theoreticians of communism. But it is very likely that he would have read Reich [16]. During the 60s, Reich's works were translated into all the major languages, but already Gary had sensed and understood enough to reject the institution of the family and to want to experiment with something new. Those were the years of the 'communes', of the 'open relationships', and Gary's behaviour towards women must be examined in this context - not in order to justify it but to understand the extent to which Gary was a true son of the sixties.

Against this same background, we have to study Gary's experimentation with drugs, because his use of such substances *was* purely experimental. In those years, the use of 'soft' drugs such as marijuana, as the symbol of rebellion, saw a rapid rise in popularity. As a principle, Gary had a puritanical abhorrence of drugs, but was attracted to the

[15] Friedrich Engels, *The origin of the family, of private property and of the State (1884)*

[16] Wilhelm Reich, *The sexual revolution (1936)*

transformation these softer drugs represented. He experimented with marijuana and was not fond of it, but was very interested in mescalin, which instead of giddiness and euphoria, gave the sensation of enhanced lucidity. He saw the drug as an instrument to help him reach the state of clarity which normally escaped him when he strove to understand his goals, the direction his life was leading. He was so enthusiastic about mescalin that he wanted to share this experience with the women he loved. From America he sent an envelope containing mescalin to Claude and Marie with detailed instructions on how to make the ´trip´. Claude, ever rigid to her principles and endowed with common sense, although sometimes to excess, not only refused to experiment with this drug, but wrote a ringing reprimand to Gary. This caused much resentment on his part, and many arguments by letter. Marie, however, tried the drug, but her fragile nature would not tolerate such an experiment, and she became quite ill. Fortunately for her, she did not experience the often addictive hallucinations.

However, it is important to understand the spirit of research in which Gary approached his experiments with hallucinations. His diaries during those years are full of poems and short texts written under the influence of mescalin or LSD. They are senseless and delirious pieces and his handwriting was often illegible. And his experiments often proved a source of frustration as the truth he believed he had grasped while in a state of hallucination, crumbled on contact with the real world.

Gary was not addicted to drugs. He was aware that the state of total, enhanced lucidity and understanding he sought in the hallucinations was nothing more than an illusion. Drugs were not even a habit for Gary, but purely an experiment, an instrument for research, just as with the mountain, his adventures, which would help him reach his goal, transcend his immediate reality.

Some stories of Gary's death which circulated in alpinist groups in Europe talked of drug abuse. In those years, drugs were naturally connected with the new thinking and radical movements in America; and thus with climbing in America, the revolution, Berkeley and Woodstock. It is therefore not surprising that this rumour, wherever it had its origin, was immediately accepted. It was the most simple explanation of all, and was perfectly befitting the death of a hero of the sixties.

CHAPTER SIXTEEN

Premonitions of Death

The hallucinations brought on by Gary's use of drugs played an important role in the events which led to his death. The 'enhanced conscious state' which Gary believed he reached, led him to reflect deeply on his own character and his relationships with others. After his initial 'trips' with mescalin, his diaries and letters reveal thoughts of death, ideas and anticipation which appeared ever more frequently in his writings. During this same period his feelings of responsibility grew stronger. Abstract discourses on his responsibility towards others would often move on to an examination of his conscience. He would go over at length his responsibilities towards his son and Claude, and even created an obligation towards Marie. Her long absence had allowed Gary's love for her to grow into something sublime. He talked of her as his wife - a 'mystical wife', and although he no longer dreamed of her joining him, he was determined to 'save' her from the 'baleful' influence of her family, to help her "discover her independence and assert her personality".

During this time, Gary also thought often of his childhood and began to miss his mother: until this point, he had been content with their infrequent correspondence. Gary's mother and her second husband had moved to Hawaii a couple of years previously. By then, despite their maturity, they were nonetheless involuntary heirs to the American pioneer tradition - so when the American government offered land in Hawaii to be cultivated for those willing to move there, they accepted without hesitation. The land they moved to was far from pleasant, in an area of marshy forests; a far cry from the cinematic scenes portraying an image of young athletic men embracing beautiful girls dressed only in flower garlands. Carmen's husband travelled there first and she followed soon after. Before returning to Europe, Gary travelled to Hawaii to visit them and stayed there for some time. This was to be the last time he would see his mother.

Carmen's move to Hawaii was one of many during her life. Her family moved from the state of Washington to Ohio, and from Ohio to California, and there must have been innumerable moves in the family history. The state of Washington, on the north-west Pacific coast, was one of the last states to be colonised, and Carmen's grandparents and great-grandparents most probably arrived there on horse-drawn wagons, having crossed the prairies of the Mid West and the Rocky Mountains.

It is important to keep in mind Gary's family history in order to understand his eternal need for movement, his mental and physical searching for open spaces. Among his family history there is for instance the tale of his Uncle

Danny and Jack London - another restless Californian who took his own life.

Migration and wandering are strong American traditions, and are the subject of a large part of classical literature. Gary was an avid reader, and would often assume various thoughts and modes of behaviour from his readings. Besides London, his favourite American authors were Mark Twain, Melville, Thoreau, John Muir, Upton Sinclair, Steinbeck and Hemingway, and at a later date, Henry Miller. These are all authors who wrote of journeys, adventures, seasonal migrations and vagabonds. (Strangely enough Gary was not fond of Kerouak, despite his resemblance to Dean Moriarty, the main character of *On the Road*.) Gary did not think of himself as linked to the underground American culture; he did not feel like a beatnik or hipster. He believed that he had travelled alone on the road as a form of personal dissent and existential research. And rather than feeling close to the metropolitan beat he would have felt more affinity with the hobo of the dancing people, the Woody Guthrie of *Bound for Glory*.

****

After the violence from the cowboys in Jackson Hole, Gary spent over one month in hospital, and this cost him a fortune. He had to borrow money from most of his friends (which he paid back in time - he was very scrupulous with regard to his borrowings, even if he had to borrow more money in order to pay back the longest debts). And so he decided to leave the States for the last time. He lingered for some time, visiting all his friends, relatives, the places he loved best, in a kind of drawn-out farewell pilgrimage.

He was disappointed with the life his relatives lived in California, and more than ever felt his estrangement with the boredom of a calm, regulated middle-class life, with all its trappings, but so lacking in intellectual stimuli. However, he did enjoy visiting his friends. He stayed for a couple of months with Yvon Chouinard and helped out in the workshop, forging climbing pegs. Gary enjoyed physical work and spent a peaceful time in Ventura with Chouinard, whose company he particularly appreciated. He had not talked of the mountains for some time, but with Chouinard this was a frequent topic. They planned various ascents and Gary returned to his project of completing his book on free climbing in California, which he would finish when he got back to France. He even obtained help from climbing photographers - Tom Frost, Ed Cooper, Harry Daley - who were to send him photographs for the book. He worked for Yvon Chouinard in order to save some money to pay his debts accumulated while in hospital, and this took some time. He also wanted to earn money in order to take out a life insurance policy, so that, in the event of his death, Lauren´s future would be assured.

He was also worried about Marie - what would become of her if he died? She would never be able to get free from her parents, would remain for ever their victim and possession. He considered making her co-beneficiary of the policy.

And then there was Maria Elena ... In the winter, when he was still on crutches and still had pains in his jaw, Gary had travelled to Baja California in Mexico for a few weeks. This journey was meant to help his injuries to mend, but was foremost a nostalgic farewell to familiar and well-loved territory. In Villa Constitución he saw a woman with a whole tribe of small children, among which was a 5-year-old girl who Gary believed to have a striking resemblance to Marie. Maria Elena was in fact, very small, thin, with a frightened look, just like the Marie Gary met for the first time in Chamonix. The young child's dark, smooth hair with her fringe reaching down to her large dark eyes strengthened the similarity.

Gary took numerous photographs of the child and spent much time talking with her and her mother. He got it into his mind that the child had great spiritual and mental qualities, and that it was his duty to help her grow and study. He fantasised about adopting her and providing for her education together with Marie. He did not think of his own son, who had the best teacher possible in Claude, but instead, providing for Maria Elena's future became of great importance for him, and he tried to convince Marie to promise to take care of her. But then his return to Europe weakened his resolve, and he eventually forgot his obsession for the child.

Before returning to France, he travelled to England, and spent a couple of months working on a road-building site in the Lake District - working out in the open and well-paid - the kind of work Gary liked and needed. In France he stopped a long while in Paris. He slept in friends' houses, or sometimes underneath the bridges over the Seine. He would go off for periods, taking various seasonal jobs - in the winter in Chamonix and other areas of Savoy they always needed people to shovel snow, and during the summer it was easy to find manual farm work or labour.

He still went to the mountains, with friends or, more often now, alone. He had overcome his fear of snow and ice and, though he thought almost daily of death, he had also overcome his fear of dying: "I am already almost without the sensation of fear; death no longer holds any real terror for me. I will shortly see if this is true when I go to Chamonix and climb a few things: I will see if I have really lost my fear of death."

How better to confirm his victory over fear than with a solo ascent? A striking, unique opportunity to exorcise his fear and to nurture the development of a desire to take his own life: "A solo ascent on a magnificent mountain, extremely dangerous and difficult (...) I have but to put on my boots, take my axe and begin just over there or there or there. The weather is good, no one would try and stop me (...) and there might be some chance of my even succeeding if I chose one easy enough. Here I can play Russian Roulette with one to 6 bullets in the chamber depending upon my mood."

By this time, thoughts of suicide appear more and more frequently in his diaries. He nursed this idea with growing fervour. One diary entry reads: "An aesthetic death. The only thing that can compensate for a ruined life."

During his last summers in Chamonix, Gary climbed with Lothar Mauch. They made up a strange rope party: Gary with his patched clothes and Lothar, who worked as a model for male fashion magazines. However when he was climbing with Gary, he tried to copy his appearance. Lothar was good company. He was younger than Gary, and fascinated by Gary's personality. He complied with all Gary's choices, and in his decision not to talk of the ascents they made. Also he accepted that Gary would often disappear for days on end, when away on his solo climbs of which nothing is known - apart from the two famous climbs of 1966, the Couloir Couturier and the north face of the Triolet. Gary grew ever more restless, and ever more inclined to solitude.

From time to time he would travel to the Calanques, where he could often find peace of mind. He had managed to find transport on a fishing boat to the island of Riou, a small, barren island bristling with limestone pinnacles, off the coast of Marseilles. He would hitch-hike from Paris, with a small present for the fisherman's daughter, and a small supply of milk and dried fruits in his rucksack. Once on the island, he would camp in a cave some ten metres above the sea. The island was, and still is, uninhabited. It is owned by the Ministry of Defence and access is not permitted. However, one person lived there: Jean Troude, or Jean de Riou, as people call him even today. He was a veteran of the Indo-China war and had found it too difficult to go back to normal life in Marseilles. Probably he had never liked life in a city, and was only happy on the deserted island. He had obtained a kind of official permit to live there, and had built a tiny shelter, which was his house. He had designated himself as guardian of the island. Despite his possessiveness towards the island and his solitude, he accepted Gary, with whom he eventually developed a close friendship. They spent many long evenings together, hardly talking, but feeling that they understood each other perfectly. Even today, if you talk to

Jean about Gary he may break down in tears: any friend of Gary's is welcomed into his house, and he would offer them his every possession.

Jean de Riou has told of Gary spending the days climbing the pinnacles on the island, solo and with no rope. On the walls of the large towers, Rébuffat and other climbers from Marseilles had opened routes, but it is quite probable that, during this period, Gary opened new ascents of which no one knows.

Only a few years earlier, Gary would have scrupulously prepared for climbs, and achieved them with famous rope partners. This was all a part of Gary's plans to "become a great alpinist". But with this change in Gary's life, it becomes extremely difficult to understand what role climbing played for him: was it still some form of initiation rite which he felt he had to repeat time and time again, or was he simply playing Russian roulette?

CHAPTER SEVENTEEN

Me - An Alpinist?

There are many who find it difficult to believe that Gary could have made ascents - and opened new routes - without talking about them, simply because this was not normal. Having your name connected with an ascent is a strong force in climbing, sometimes stronger than any other motivation. And Gary did want to climb new routes, and for his achievements to be known. He had dreamed of becoming a great alpinist, but then, suddenly, this was no longer of any importance, and his climbing changed totally. After the rescue on the Dru, he would often reply to journalists who referred to him as an alpinist: "Me, an alpinist? I'm an adventurer." He said that he admired Walter Bonatti above all other alpinists "because he sought adventure", and he emphasised that by adventure he meant research; of all aspects and in every direction.

However, the fact remains that Gary Hemming, for those who remember him, was an alpinist; a controversial alpinist who was valued by many, overrated according to others.

He was not highly admired in the States; having been absent during the years of the great ascents in Yosemite at the end of the 50s, his name was not connected with any famous routes. His achievements in the Alps were not talked of in his home country, and American climbers who did not travel to the Alps, did not consider him worthy of note. It is important to recognise that initially Gary suffered from several weak points with regard to climbing: he was afraid of climbing on wet rock, not to mention his fear of snow and ice. It took him many seasons in the Alps to overcome these fears. On his own admission, during the majority of climbs on snow-covered rock with John Harlin, his only thought was to get to the top safely, and often he was not able to enjoy the actual climbing. But then he gained confidence on snow, to the extent that he climbed solo on ice walls and mixed terrain. However, it is not surprising that American climbers, like Steve Roper, who had only done some minor ascents in Yosemite with Gary, did not believe him to be a great climber.

Sterling Neale and Charles Plummer remember climbing with Gary on Orizaba in Mexico, when Gary complained bitterly, and appeared to have difficulties on relatively easy snow fields. That day, however, none of them were fit. They all developed severe headaches and Briggs and Dunnagan did not even make it to the summit. However, Sterling and Charles were astonished when they later heard of Gary's ascents in the Alps.

His other friends from the Tetons remember him as a good climber, but not exceptional. Barry Corbet remembers that when Gary first arrived in the Tetons, they had all been very impressed by him and believed him to be some kind of superman, mostly because he knew all the famous characters from Yosemite, the 'Gunks and other areas. Afterwards, however, they came to realise that the well-known climbers from Yosemite and the 'Gunks knew little of Hemming, and did not consider him to be part of their group. Gary was then certainly a good climber, as with all the guides in the Tetons, but nothing more than that. However, the 'big boss' of the Tetons guides, Glenn Exum, remembers Gary as a good alpinist and an excellent guide.

His friends from his first years of climbing, such as Dick Long and Jerry Gallwas, talk of Gary as talented and most of all, reliable. Long told me: "I've always thought that if anything went wrong in the mountains, Gary would have been able to cope". Layton Kor, who climbed with Gary in Joshua Tree, at Tahquitz and who met Gary in the Alps, believes that he was an excellent climber and a good alpinist.

Tom Frost remembers that Gary's climbing abilities changed with his moods. He could be the best or the worst climber in the world, changing from day to day. However, on the Fou with Frost, Gary had climbed excellently. He had lead several pitches and shown no sign of fear or insecurity. In Joshua Tree, where they went to take photographs for Gary's book on Californian climbing techniques, Gary did not want to appear in the photographs: as if he was not capable of climbing or was too modest. "He had the inherent ability to lead, to make others follow."

"He had imagination," Royal Robbins recalls Gary on the *American Direct* on the Dru, "and he always found the right people to accompany him on the routes he had conceived." According to Robbins, Gary was an excellent companion and a very good climber.

Even René Desmaison pays tribute to Gary's ingenious, intuitive ideas and remarkable qualities as an alpinist. In Europe Gary was generally admired. He often discussed with his French friends his opinion that they were too superficial in their safety techniques, and too ´primitive´ in their climbing techniques (the French climbers, for their part, accused him of excessive refinement of movements, and a mania for safety which often resulted in a slow pace). Despite the criticism, however, he was an extremely popular figure. For the French he had become a type of national hero and it is therefore not surprising that they were unable to judge him objectively, and that later - after his death - Gary became a legend even in other alpine countries.

Gary had many friends also in Great Britain. He liked British climbers because they climbed in a fashion in sympathy with his theories. Each time he visited Great Britain, he would take time to travel as far north as the Lake District and Scotland to go climbing. Unfortunately, Stewart Fulton and Mick Burke who knew him best, cannot tell us their opinions of Gary as climber and friend: Burke disappeared very close to the summit of Everest and Fulton, who was an electrician by trade, was electrocuted and killed while at work. Don Whillans talked of Gary as a skilled, downright daring climber. Others, such as Chris Bonington and John Cleare, believe that the Hemming's abilities as an alpinist were somewhat exaggerated as a result of the legendary status he achieved. However, they had never climbed with him: they had seen him only together with Harlin, and anyone in Harlin's shadow would find it difficult to shine. Ken Wilson remembers in particular Gary's technical research of climbing gear, and Dennis Gray was impressed by the fact that, rather than discuss mountaineering, Gary was very interested in talking of the problems which were threatening the very survival of the earth, such as pollution. These subjects are common today, but were completely unknown during the sixties.

It is not surprising that there are so many contrasting opinions about Gary Hemming's abilities as an alpinist. His changes of temperament were often so great that they had to influence his performance in the mountains. However, in order to become a legend, you have to do more than excel in one discipline.

For those who did not know Hemming, and have only heard about him, he was the climber of the *American Direct* of the Dru and the south face of the Fou, but most of all he was the Californian who introduced the concept of ΄ecological΄ climbing to the Alps (using chocks and slings for safety, or if using pegs, removing them after use).

And so the legend of Gary Hemming was created around his role as innovator, and was enhanced by his image as a 60s icon, and the events which captured the public's imagination - the rescue on the Dru - and his romantic death.

It would be interesting to hear what John Harlin thought of Gary Hemming as an alpinist. It is safe to say that he was aware of Gary's abilities, as he would often seek out Gary to accompany him on a climb, and as they had so many major projects in common. At a certain point, Gary stopped climbing with John, but continued to visit him in Leysin, where John had founded a climbing school - the famous International School of Modern Mountaineering (ISMM) - where the instructors were the crème de la crème of international climbing. Gary stopped climbing with John because he did not approve of John's way of 'attacking' a mountain, and he disagreed with the excessive publicity around John's first ascents. John had no difficulty in finding new climbing companions, but the fact remains that together they were a formidable climbing team.

As for John Harlin, all those who climbed with him agree that he was in a class above the rest, the best of them all.

CHAPTER EIGHTEEN

John

John's death was a hard blow for Gary. Since they had stopped climbing together, all feelings of rivalry had disappeared, leaving behind the strength of a friendship built up over many years. John was the only old friend Gary had in Europe, and the only person with whom Gary had a past in common. Since the Harlins moved to Leysin, Gary went to visit them often, with Claude and Lauren. Sometimes, when Gary was away, Claude would go there just with Lauren, and spend some days with Mara and her children. The two women had developed a close friendship: both intelligent, well-educated and both loved their work (Mara was a biologist and taught at the American School in Leysin), and both had to play the difficult role of mother to children whose father had other things on his mind. In John's mind, the most predominant thought was the Eiger.

The north face of the Eiger, which John had managed to climb with Konrad Kirch, after numerous attempts, remained a source of primary fascination for John. This is understandable when you take into consideration John's temperament: he was only interested in going to the most extreme of extremes, and as the Eiger then represented extreme danger and extreme difficulty, all attempts on the Eiger were for John the embodiment of extreme audacity. In short, the north face of the Eiger was John's ideal of mountaineering.

Furthermore, John was fascinated by a new approach introduced during those years by the Germans, which was immediately taken up by all those climbing at the upper limits in the Alps. This method demanded a direttissima ascent, choosing a route up a vertical line, ´as the water drops´, irrespective of any logical route following the ´weaknesses´ of a face such as cracks or ribs.

John had begun to think of a direttissima route immediately after having climbed the classic route on the north face, and had been on a reconnoitring trip in 1963. In 1964, he returned to the face in February to attempt this new route in winter (this was to be the second - the original route had already been climbed in the winter of 1961 by a German party led by Toni Hiebeler). John's winter attempt failed due to poor weather conditions. He tried once again in the summer with four Italians (Piussi and Sorgato, whom he had met during his previous ascent, and Buonafede and Menegus) together with two Frenchmen, Desmaison and Bertrand. They bivouacked on the face for four nights and succeeded in climbing further than on John´s previous attempt. However, once again, they were forced to turn back because of bad weather.

The north face of the Eiger is infamous for its sudden, cruel storms brought about by the thick clouds that often gather against this two thousand metre high rock and ice face, that almost blocks the head of the valley. And with these storms come hailstones and snow, making any form of progress impossible. All the tragedies witnessed by this cruel face have been brought about by bad weather, and all failed attempts have been blocked suddenly by the change in weather conditions.

John began to think of the possibility of attempting the ´very direct´ route in winter. During this season, days are shorter but changes in weather are not as great. The cold would of course be extreme: though this was a problem in itself, it would provide better safety in that the infamous loose rock and avalanche-prone snow feared by all who attempted the face, would be made more stable by winter's icy conditions.

John met a Scot, Dougal Haston, who had climbed the north face by the classic route in 1963, and involved him in his project. In the winter of 1964, they carried out a reconnaissance of the face. There was a lot of fresh snow, and the difficulties encountered on the first pitch were graded at VI.

John made a new attempt in the summer of '65, but failed, and turned instead to the direttissima on the west face of the Petit Dru. He had already attempted this route with Lito Tejada-Flores during the previous summer, and then once again with Pierre Mazeaud and Roberto Sorgato. Finally he completed the new route with Royal Robbins. Then during the first days of February 1966, John returned to the Eiger with a group of very talented climbers, determined to open the ´very direct´ before the end of the winter. With him were Dougal Haston and Layton Kor, a tall Californian, skilled in artificial climbing and in climbing on friable rock, from long experience in the Arizona and Californian deserts. Chris Bonington, one of the foremost English alpinists of that time, was also in the group, but taking part only as support and official photographer. (But, having Bonington along was for John a big safety bonus.) Later on they were joined by another skilled English climber, Don Whillans, for a couple of weeks. When they arrived at the Kleine Scheidegg, the hotel facing the immense rock face, they were met with the news that eight Germans were also attempting the direttissima route.

The full story of the ascent is given in detail in two books [17], and therefore does not need to be repeated. It is a story of short pitches conquered day by day, hammering in pegs, fixing ropes to be jumared every morning, and proceeding from where they stopped the evening before. The same operations were shadowed by the Germans, only a few metres to one side of Harlin's route. There were long intervals when bad weather forced everyone to descend, leaving their ropes fixed on the face. It is also a very sad story, as John, who had faced much greater dangers on other mountains and even on the Eiger, fell and was killed.

He died, falling free over one thousand metres, turning through the air his arms wide open, like some angel - those watching the face with binoculars from the Kleine Scheidegg saw him fall. His death was brought about by a bizarre accident, at that time unforeseeable; however, his death, with its widespread consequences and the controversial discussions it provoked, contributed to shedding some light on the problem of how to use fixed ropes, reascending them by a jumar system [18]. And to some

[17] P. Gillman and D. Haston, *Eiger Direct*, London 1966 an account of the ascent. J.R. Ullman, *Straight Up*, New York 1968: the biography of John Harlin.

extent, his death may have helped to save the lives of others who would go on to use the same technique, but would avoid such a fatal error.

John was reascending the face on a rope. In front of him were Dougal Haston and one of the Germans, who had already reached the rest point on the snow field, called the Spider (by that point, the rivalry between the two parties had been abandoned and they had agreed to work together). John was hanging over thin air on the second to last rope, which the two before him had already climbed, when it broke. It was a perlon rope 7 mm in diameter. This was not too thin, as some have claimed - a rope used in this way only has to bear the weight of one man, not the sudden strain of a fall, and does not therefore have to be too thick. But this rope was made of perlon. John and Dougal had chosen it with care, as they did with all the other gear. The new perlon ropes were lighter but more durable and elastic than the old hemp ropes, and even the nylon ropes. They were known to be extremely valuable for safety in the mountains as their elastic nature could absorb a sudden strain in the event of a fall to a much higher degree than other less resilient ropes. But this elasticity proved fatal for John. They had not foreseen that such a rope would naturally stretch when ascended, then contract when the climber's weight left the rope. This meant that the rope was continuously rubbing against the rock causing constant wear and the risk of breaking. The rope which broke under John's weight was fixed over an overhang and had rubbed against its rocky edge. It had been used for several reascents, and having stretched and contracted, it had rubbed against the edge hundreds of times. It had held

[18] By way of small fiction knots or some mechanical gripping device.

the weight of Dougal, the Germans, of John himself and all the others, before it broke - fate decided John's death.

****

Gary saw John's death as a premonition of his own. He did not believe in accidental death, and had always maintained that if someone died in an accident, it was because they wanted to die, or because they did not have enough will to live. He had in fact come to believe that death, however it happened, was a voluntary act.

"More and more I am becoming convinced that we do not die accidentally or by sickness but we die by personal choice via subconscious self destruction or conscious desire for the experience of death."

But how could John have had a conscious or subconscious desire for death? He was the embodiment of nature's forces, of a love for life. Gradually, Gary imposed his state of mind and feelings of guilt upon John's fate. He became convinced that John's subconscious fall towards death was caused by a desire to punish himself, for his guilt in wanting to own, to possess the Eiger, by means of brute force.

"What died, what really was killed last week? Something died, of that I am certain. What was it? You went against certain rules of conduct - or no, not against, because in essence there is nothing against nothing in the universe. When we attempt to go against a force so absolutely your superior one is bent into another direction perhaps but it's certainly not against you that the force reverts. It is you that is against you when you fail to take into consideration this force. Anyway the only thing certain is that John failed to climb his ideal by a fashion beneath him (.....) tying up the Eiger with ropes and the strength of mechanical rigs to possess his ideal under the most unidealistic manners."

But being able to explain someone's death, and accepting it are two completely different tasks, and Gary could not accept John's death. He did not go to Leysin for the funeral, and wrote and rewrote a letter to Mara innumerable times before sending it. For days on end, he thought over John's death, connecting it to his personal fate, and consequently rejecting his friend's death: "And John? His so called death. Is it real? What has really happened to his becoming? How does one become anything after he loses all physical contact with the world?" Eventually, Gary totally rejected John's death, and began to imagine climbing with John that next summer.

"John is one of my dearest friends. His death I refuse to accept and so far as I am concerned he is still very much alive; you can interpret that as you please but his fall from the Eiger last week means that I cannot climb alone next summer. I have spoken with him about this and because of our long past together, because of our friendship, I must do these climbs with him. It should be a marvellous season because I think we'll get on like we never ever could before and his belay will be of the greatest aid to me (...)

"You John are my best mate. It is to you I give the reign. You pick the climb and the time and we'll be off and away with them (...)

"You know like that night in Oregon years ago when we climbed by the light of the moon those pinnacles along the side of the road. That was a special night for me, to be sure. And we each picked our own route and each was independent of the other, and yet we were still one another's assurance. An assurance without rope or speech but presence. That's the best way for us to climb the summer, John - each in solo and you come along whenever you please and you leave whenever you please. That's the best way certainly."

CHAPTER NINETEEN

Transitional Years

The years following John's death were transitional years, an anticipation of Gary's fate, the grande finale that Gary was constantly waiting for, without knowing whether it would bring happiness or death. Those next three years were not uneventful, but by then Gary was on the path towards his own destiny, and accepted events rather than provoking them.

During the summer of 1966 he did several magnificent climbs on the Mont Blanc massif, attached in his mind to John's rope. On these climbs he experienced the feelings of joy and fearlessness that by now he always felt when climbing since his return from the States.

It was the summer of the rescue on the Dru.

That summer saw also Gary's passion for Marie die down. He had spent all the spring tormenting her, but by that time, Marie had grown up, was engaged to another - whom she later married - and finally was able to find the words to tell Gary that she was not his wife, that she did not want to read his diaries, and that she wanted him to leave her alone. It took Gary months to get over this news, and in truth he never really resigned himself to losing her. Among the thousands of books he had read, he had stumbled across the stories of King Arthur, and discovered that he had the same name, Gareth, as one of the king's knight. He grew to love these stories, and wanted to show them to Marie (who really was not at all interested). Marie was now his Lynette or Lyonette, the name of Gareth's lady. Poor Gary! It seems incredible that on the eve of 1968, when everyone was reading Marcuse and Lévy-Strauss, the 'beatnik of the Alps' should spend his nights poring over *Morte d'Arthur* [19], and copying Gareth's poem from *Idylls of the King* by Tennyson for Marie [20].

He made one last attempt that summer to see Marie, climbing over the hedge of her parents' house in Fonteney-les-Roses - the occasion when he was arrested. But then, gradually, he became resigned to her rejection and his thoughts were otherwise occupied. Already that spring he had met Françoise, Colette and Marie Laure. He moved around between these three women. Then, after his face was on the front page of all the newspapers, he began to receive numerous letters from female admirers, and replied to some of them. He met many other women, fell in love, had a great time, then grew tired of them.

Initially Gary did not like Françoise who he found annoying; but gradually, she became very important. Claude believes that she was probably the right woman for Gary, a kind of compromise between Claude and Marie. She was more mature than Marie and more adventurous than Claude; she could have followed Gary on his

[19] Sir Thomas Malory, *Morte d'Arthur* 1485

[20] Lord Alfred Tennyson, *Idylls of the King* 1885

wanderings and made him happy.

Towards the end of 1966, Gary went back on his resolve and returned to the States. This was a short journey, only lasting one month, and Gary's travel and accommodation were paid for by his publisher so that he could get enough photographs for his book on Free Climbing in California. He stayed for a while with Schlief in La Mesa, and in San Francisco with Gail, one of his first girlfriends before he left for Europe. He went to Joshua Tree with Tom Frost to take photographs for the instructional part of the book. Ed Cooper and Henry Daley gave him some photographs, and he even managed to get some photographs from Ansel Adams and Jim Bridwell.

When he returned to Paris he was greeted with an offer of work on television. A producer had been impressed by his face and offered him the part of King Harold in a adaptation produced by French television on the conquest of England. A tragic hero! The ideal role for Gary. He really enjoyed playing the part, liked the world of television and became even more popular when he appeared on the screen in a long tunic, his blond hair down to his shoulders and his hollow face, that of an ascetic. However, his face in truth showed the signs of someone who was ´burning the candle at both ends´.

This was a time of intense work for Gary. He lived in the apartment provided by his publisher and worked simultaneously on two books - the Californian climbing book and *Patchwork of Research*. The climbing book demanded a great deal of checking and research, and Gary went to Leysin to consult Robbins, who had taken Harlin's place in the management of the climbing school. Robbins provided much assistance. He liked and admired Hemming, and moreover, was interested in the subject. Gary taped six hours of conversations with Robbins on the technical and ethical problems connected with climbing. He started on the task of transcribing the tapes, but then his other project took over and for several months Gary worked only on *Patchwork of Research*.

He spent the summer in Chamonix, arriving with some girlfriend. Then Claude arrived and then he met other women. They made him lose time, made him feel trapped. Was this a mistake to give up so much time to women or just an excuse because he was no longer interested in climbing? He left Chamonix in the middle of August: "Chamonix is not the right place for you, Gary. Fame has unbalanced you. Chamonix and its mountains in summer are not for you. You need to be alone. You will not find solitude in a place like this."

There were also journalists in Chamonix who tried to get interviews with Gary: "Journalists want to produce some image for their readers, all black or all white. I'm lucky! they still are painting me in white. It's all very nice, but not the truth, and you come to the point when the lack of truth grows into a heavy burden to bear."

Gary escaped to the Calanques, but even his favourite place was not quiet in August. So it was back to Paris, to work ...

Gary's life became frenetic, and the footprints he left behind become unclear, are lost.

CHAPTER TWENTY

Last Journey to Jackson

Barry Corbet told me that Gary went to Sweden with
Françoise in the spring of 1968 in order to attend a
University course in Stockholm or Malmö. The details of
this trip are not known as Gary's diaries from his last two
years have been lost and Françoise has disappeared. Barry
remembers Gary telling him that during the journey to
Sweden, they spent the time pretending to be different
characters, playing a role as if in some theatrical play.

They had not been together long. Barry remembers
that it took Gary a very long courtship to win her affections,
and that at the start, she was inflexible. It is possible that
the Françoise he knew before the rescue on the Dru was
another woman. It is known, however, that Gary and
Françoise were together in 1968, and that they went to
Sweden together.

They also spent some time in Chamonix, staying in
an attic in the Hotel de Paris. Gary took up several small
jobs; in winter shovelling snow from the roofs of the large
hotels, secured by a rope tied to the chimney. Françoise

worked in the hotel serving breakfast. Lou Janin, who was at that time the owner of the Hotel de Paris, remembers the couple as very scrupulous and careful not to take advantage of his hospitality: one morning Françoise was ill and could not come down to serve breakfast - Gary did not eat in the hotel as he normally did because "he did not have the right".

They made plans for the future, or maybe the plans were only Gary's. He wanted to go to the Himalaya with Françoise and they needed money. Françoise was offered a job in the French Embassy in Nairobi, and while she was preparing to leave, Gary travelled to Alaska, where he got work on an oil pipeline site in Fairbanks. This was tough work in unpleasant surroundings, but well-paid. Gary made no friends, did not go climbing, but just worked. Then he went back on his promise for a second time, and before returning to Europe, he stopped off in the States.

In May 1968, Barry Corbet was involved in an accident. He had specialised in filming mountaineering, and during a take of a ski race in Colorado, the helicopter from which he was filming crashed and Barry suffered severe injuries to his spinal cord.

No one knows when Gary heard this news, but we can presume that it was at some point in 1968, because Gary's friends used to write to him from time to time. He may have known about it when he got back from Sweden, but he had no plans to return to the States at that time. However, the following year, on his way back from Alaska, he travelled directly to Denver to visit Barry, who went to meet him at the airport in a wheelchair.

Barry does not like to think back over those two and a half weeks when Gary tried with all his might to cure Barry of his ´intolerable condition´. It is certain that for Gary, the thought of his friend being stuck in a wheelchair would seem more unbearable than death itself. "He worked very hard and with great determination," tells Barry, "as he alone could." Obviously his treatment had no medical or scientific background, but Gary had such belief in his efforts that it is really quite incredible that he did not succeed.

Barry prefers not to talk about it and can only say that it was a terrible time. After two and a half weeks of exhaustive efforts to get Barry to walk by sheer will power (Gary's naturally, which he tried to transmit to Barry), Gary pointed a pistol at Barry's temple and ordered him to stand up. Barry raised himself on his arms and fell to the ground - what else could he do? But then Gary emptied the magazine of the revolver, put one bullet back in, and spun it round ...

But Barry does not like to talk about that time.

Gary took his role of saviour very seriously, and grew frustrated by his own impotence. He was also shocked and deeply upset by the confirmation that Barry was powerless against his injuries. Of all his friends, Gary probably had most admiration for Barry, and he could not accept that a man of such mental and moral strength was not able to ´dominate his situation´ and overcome a purely physical problem.

Still today - twenty-four years on and after all those years in a wheelchair - Barry Corbet radiates an extraordinary sense of strength and confidence. This was how Gary saw him, and it was perhaps seeing his friend deprived of this inner strength during the time after his accident that upset Gary most.

Eventually he left Denver and travelled to the Tetons to visit his old friends. Barry's ex-wife, Muffy, had come to visit Barry. She was also leaving for Jackson Hole with her oldest son, and Gary joined them. Muffy had a small log cabin near Wilson, outside Jackson in the middle of a forest near the mountains. Gary immediately liked this spot and stayed there for a couple of weeks. He shared the cabin with Muffy and Barry's three children, who he took for walks through the forest, sang 'The Yellow Submarine' with them and told them adventure stories. Also he talked to them about his own son. He had a teddy bear with him for Lauren and he set up small shows pretending that the teddy bear was Lauren and he was the father telling him stories. Muffy remembers watching the first men on the moon on television with Gary - so it must have been July.

Gary spent much time talking with Muffy. The many months he had spent working alone had made him want to confide in someone - unusual for Gary. He had always liked Muffy, an attractive woman with red hair, who had flirted with Gary while she was between marriages - she had been married to Barry twice and they had got divorced twice. However, Gary had never told her anything about himself, but during these discussions he told her about his life in Europe, about Claude and Lauren. He talked about Françoise and their plans, and even told her of events far back in his childhood and adolescence - events he had never recounted to anyone before and which were not even mentioned in his diaries. One of these occurred when he was eleven years old and staying in the countryside near La Mesa and three grown men had tried to rape him. He told Muffy that after this terrible experience, he developed an uncontrollable fear of men. This emotion was never apparent in the adult Gary, but it could provide an explanation for his sudden and incomprehensible bouts of aggression which were, maybe, some instinctive form of self-defence. It is also probable that his fear of America, his fear of the violence provoked in him by being in America, can be traced back to this distant event.

Gary travelled between Wilson, Jackson and Jenny Lake, visiting friends. That summer was beautiful and most of his friends were there, whether in tents or in the wooden cabins (which were later taken down by the National Park authorities).

He called Peggy in Colorado and asked her to join them in the Tetons. Peggy could not make it at the time, or maybe she did not want to go. When talking about that day now, she still breaks down in tears: "If only I'd known ... Maybe he needed me. Maybe I could have helped him ..."

So many of Gary's friends say "If only I'd known ..." But how could they have known? Gary seemed so alive and well, his trip back to the States renewing all his energy. He was the Gary they had always known - noisy, warm-hearted, encroaching, but then suddenly disappearing to go off somewhere to think - just as he always had done. He went to visit Pete Sinclair who was in Jackson with his wife and three children, the youngest just born. Gary played with the children, and apologised to Connie, to whom he had been very rude during his last visit. He was always rude to his friends' wives, who he accused of trapping their husbands. Connie had grown angry with his sarcastic remarks and had hit him over the head with a heavy electric torch. Gary respected her reaction and from that moment on held her in great admiration.

Charles Plummer, the old ´Carlos´, was also staying with Pete, and was leaving for Seattle. Gary and he went to visit Sterling Neale and his ex-wife Lynn. They spent an enjoyable afternoon drinking beer and reminiscing over their travels in Mexico.

Gary also went to visit Willi Unsoeld. They talked of the 1963 Everest expedition, the first successful American expedition to reach the highest peak in the world, when Unsoeld (with Tom Hornbein) had made the first ascent of the West Ridge and the first traverse of the mountain (supported by Barry Corbet). They talked of absent friends from the Tetons - of Jake Breitenbach killed on Everest, and of Barry Corbet, also on the expedition - talented, strong, generous Barry, but now ...

Gary could not stop thinking about his friend stuck in a wheelchair, and of his own failure to help him. He went to talk to Bill Briggs and made him promise that after Gary left, Bill would take care of Barry and would do all he could to help him get better.

And then it was August 6th , and the ´tea party´ on the banks of Jenny Lake was arranged.

CHAPTER TWENTY-ONE

The Tea Party

As always, the tea party took place on Guide's Hill, near Jenny Lake. Most of the old crowd were there, but as the party started in the afternoon and went on until late that night, people came and went, and it is difficult to establish who was where at certain times of the day. As was the tradition, there was a lot to eat and people brought wine and beer. Gary arrived in the middle of the afternoon with Muffy. They had been in the mountains and had not eaten lunch. They sat down to table and drank a fair amount of wine. There was also lots of beer and some slivovitz which Muffy had brought with her.

Muffy remembers that Gary had been happy all morning, but, before going to the party, he had gone by the post office in Moose to see if there was any mail for him. There was none and Gary's mood changed.

Bill arrived later on, and by that point there were at least eight people there, amongst whom were two young guides, Mike Lowe and Dean Moore, just back from a day's work. Besides Muffy there were two other women: Joan, who was always following Muffy and Gary (Muffy believed that she was in love with Gary, but Gary could not bear her), and Robin, Dean Moore's wife. All of them were drinking, except for Mike who was discussing guiding in the Tetons with Dean. Muffy can remember Gary growing quite animated about this discussion - he maintained that the American system favoured exploitation and that Glenn Exum, the director of the guide service for the Tetons Park, exploited his guides. He tried to convince the guides there to join forces and rebel, and then went on to insult them, calling them cowards because they did not react. Muffy walked off with Robin half way through this discussion.

Their argument grew more and more violent. Mike Lowe got the impression that Gary was taking out some frustration on Dean and himself, creating an argument so that he could give vent to his own anger. Mike, a large, sturdy figure but with a calm nature, tried to back off from the argument - he had heard, as everyone in Jackson had, of Gary and his arguments, mostly due to the old story of the fight with the cowboys, and he did not want any trouble. Gary, however, set his sights on Mike and would not let him walk off. In order to provoke him, Gary swept off Mike´s glasses: "Stand up and fight," he shouted. Mike stood up and with one judo move, had Gary on his back.

He had no intention of hurting him, but just wanted to keep him under control.

Mike remembers that at this point, Gary began to cry on his shoulder, while others say that he began to laugh to try to play down his defeat. But the Wild West is the Wild West - and for all those who have seen the films and read the books, if you lose a fight, you are humiliated. Gary felt he had lost face in front of those present, and reacted by attacking Joan verbally. Joan could not take this - she also had drunk a lot (everyone was rather tense at that moment) - and she slapped him. At that point, Muffy returned and Gary turned his anger on her, slapping her on the face as Joan had slapped him.

Muffy ran off to her car. Gary followed her to get his rucksack which was in the car, but Muffy was frightened and locked herself in the car.

During all this, Bill had been trying to make peace, and had managed to get everyone, or almost everyone, to leave. Today, after so much time, it is difficult to be exact about events, and therefore difficult to be sure about when Gary fired a shot in the air. According to Muffy this happened before she locked herself in the car. According to Bill it was afterwards, and the others do not remember. Consequently, it is even more difficult to work out whether Gary had the pistol with him or whether it was, in fact, in his rucksack in the car. The latter version is the more probable, because we already know that Gary always had a pistol in his rucksack, and that he never used it. (His friends were shocked to hear that Gary always carried a pistol in his rucksack. When they asked him "What is it for?" Gary would reply, "You never know". During his last journey to the States, he actually had two: one he left with Barry Corbet in Denver, and a lighter one he took with him to the Tetons.) If he had left his rucksack in the car, he was not likely to take the pistol with him, having only returned from the mountains and not from a war - and he certainly did not have anywhere on his person to keep a gun.

However, much confusion surrounds this part of the evening. Mike Lowe and Dean Moore had gone off, along with Joan, so it would appear that only Gary, Muffy and Bill remained. Muffy remembers that Gary began to cry, saying that no one understood him, no one was willing to do anything, and he began to shout that the next day, he would come back and kill Glenn Exum to avenge all the guides. Then he shouted at Muffy to go or else he would kill her too. Muffy was scared and ran off to the Moore's house.

Muffy, Dean and Robin had agreed to go climbing together the next day. They got up at 6.30 a.m. A few metres from the area where the party had taken place the day before was a police car, and Gary's body lay across the path. It was covered, but they recognised him by the clogs he always wore.

This attempt at a reconstruction of the events is based mainly on the testimony of Muffy, Mike Lowe, Dean Moore and Bill Briggs. Muffy says that she had drunk quite a lot and does not remember the exact sequence of events. Mike and Dean say they remember things clearly, but left as soon as Gary turned his attention from them.

Bill has told me the story twice, once in writing.

CHAPTER TWENTY-TWO

Bill's Account

He returned from Alaska and arrived in the Tetons after staying with Corbet in Denver.

"Briggs, you've got to do something for Corbet. It's up to you!"

I had no idea what had transpired between them, only that Gary had given it his best shot, so to speak. All I could do was express my agreement that by getting around mental blocks, Barry could walk. The person has to want to, however, and who knows what the extent of the blockage might be?

We talked about his ´FAME´ and how it was undeserved and an embarrassment for him. This item he could not resolve at all and so he avoided further recognition ... almost went out of his way to do so. Reporters were creating a false image which insulted his need to be genuine. Indeed, FAME is always a tough issue to accommodate well, I find, and this is true of everyone, I think. People tend to flock around like vultures looking to grab a piece of the action. The trick is to become too big of a bite ... this works well indeed as long as it doesn't swell up one's head.

He spoke also of the guide training and examination in

Chamonix. Essentially it was an elimination race traversing several of the peaks across the valley from the Mont Blanc massif. He'd passed the first stage of guide qualification, but harboured some disagreement with the process or perhaps I was only hearing an echo of my own thoughts on the matter. Still certifications tend to be a suppressive and perhaps totally unnecessary formality, set up with the purpose of excluding rather than enabling others to be included. I don't like it and believe it leads us unnecessarily into conflict with one another. Seems to me he was approving this line of reasoning.

Finally a 'Guide's Hill' party was held wherein all manner of friends and guests were invited (approved?) to attend. Pot luck food supplied by the wives and girlfriends and alcohol by the men. It's typically an undisciplined abuse of drinking that's become a habit at most institutions of higher learning. Looking back over decades of attending such drunkenness, I conclude it is not beneficial for anyone or any group despite the feeling of brotherhood one may think it cements. Becoming a 'drinking buddy' is a very superficial basis for friendship which leads eventually to disaster - doesn't it?

Anyway I couldn't agree with getting drunk at the party, particularly in that I had clients to serve the next morning. So I had held down my intake to a moderate amount so as to not be hung over and yet enough to reduce inhibitions I've had with interpersonal communications. Night came on and the party thinned out to hard core participants.

The first indication I had that we were in for trouble was a heavy discussion just at dusk. The topic was disastrous and it had already reached an unbelievable depth of seriousness when I came over to that group (....) I understood that this was THE most upsetting (discouraging) topic anyone can get caught up in. Here was an emergency that no one else was going to recognise. I would have to re-direct it. Carefully I steered the conversation to another topic (anything would do) and to my relief it worked!

Although the topic was never again revisited, I still feel the damage was done and those participating in it for the most part did not recover. This meant that we had a difficult night (if not few days) coming up. I set about to systematically convince everyone to go home by talking with each one alone. Meanwhile Gary had gotten locked in with Joan, trying to get her to come out of her shell (or whatever). It got to the point of him slapping her before I succeeded in changing the direction. This was beginning to be a juggling act, get everyone to go home yet keep track of what's happening.

Then came a confrontation with one of the Lowe brothers. He and Gary were mutually enmeshed in belittlement such that a macho challenge ensued verbally and finally progressed to physical contact or pushing each other around. Gary went into the fire laughing as I recall, probably at the absurdity of it all. Anyway the incident dissolved with Lowe being persuaded to leave the party.

Gradually I managed to get everyone to leave and I determined I would simply stay with Gary all night, hopefully we could sleep and I'd be rested enough for my clients. It was a warm night and we laid down in the tall grass beyond the parking lot. He was pretty badly depressed, having been unable to get others to ´see´. I listened carefully and inserted positive statements whenever I could ... gains he'd made, the stars above us, our friendship, the help he'd been to me, etc. I put my arm around him and he cried a bit, then settled down to perhaps sleep.

I was patting myself on the back for having done such a good job of averting disaster when a car drove into the parking area with lights right on us. Gary was aroused, of course, and proceeded to get back into a confrontation with the girl (with whom he had been staying in Jackson). There was a marvellously funny scene where he was on the hood of the car preventing her from leaving with his nose pressed against the windshield and she turned the wipers on. He wanted his pack and for some reason she was trying to leave without him having it. Well, he got the pack or got into it at least to get out a revolver.

I was still trying to subdue the scene in my quiet, round-about way, but not succeeding. Gary fired the revolver to prove a point to her and I decided I was in the way more than helping out. So I played my final card and said I was going to bed, since they had things well in hand. They gave me stunned looks of disbelief and I trusted that meant that they realised that they were responsible now. Wrong! Obviously it didn't work: 20 minutes later (I'd say) there was a second gun shot.

I recall thinking probably Gary had committed suicide, or perhaps shot the girl; but right then it became apparent that he was right above me (I was sleeping in my van that summer). I think I initiated the communication by intending (saying) "Hi, are you all right?" He replied that he was unhappy. Glad to be rid of the body. He gave me the impression that there was something seriously wrong with the body, but did not indicate what. Just that it was a relief of major magnitude. I suggested that it's always a relief to be out of the body, but he corrected me on this to indicate he was relieved to be totally rid of that body.

He conveyed to me that he was sorry about leaving such a mess. I replied that I could handle the body, etc. all OK. Not that, the messes in Europe! and Denver! and in Africa! [21] *No matter, these can be worked out too, I reassured him. I would see to it. He expressed his appreciation and I returned to the flow, meaning*

[21] In order to be exact, Bill did not mention Africa in this first account, but in a second one. In another document he wrote Boulder instead of Denver: he is referring to Barry Corbet who at the time of Gary's death lived in Denver and then moved near to Boulder.

to make it known to him what a beneficial effect he'd been in my life. I was doing better and had become more able due to his lead. The feeling of affinity for one another grew very strong indeed, and we just grooved on that for a while. Finally I suggested he get on his way and I started getting about cleaning things up around here. And he was gone at once.

I got up at once, eager with curiosity. What had just transpired for me was a new experience; was it really true? The lights of the girl's car were still on, so I turned them off and closed the door. I searched around Guide's Hill to try to find her, but there was no sign of anyone awake. Could be Gary had shot her. I figured the body would be just over the hill on the entrance road and started to go check that out ... and stopped. Is it really prudent to go searching for someone with a gun, at night with only a flashlight? One could get killed needlessly. No matter what had happened, couldn't it wait until dawn? I went back to bed.

At early dawn I got up again and went straight to the place where I thought Gary's body would be... and so it was. I called the Park Service and a Ranger came quickly enough. He took my report, I got some breakfast and met my clients for the day. On returning there was the expected grieving individuals around. Some set about to console my sorrow and of course I had none! Should I tell them what had transpired? Would it do any good? I made a few attempts and gave it up. All I could get across was that I thought Gary was perhaps no worse off now. Actually I was rather sure he was MUCH better off."

This was the letter Bill Briggs sent to me when I asked for his help in my research. He replied with this detailed account of the events of that evening. When I met him in Jackson, some two years later, he was able to confirm his version of the story to me on all points.

At first I thought Bill was maybe a bit crazy with his stories of Gary's spirit hovering over him in the van, and I had rejected his account as unreliable. Later on, however, during my travels in the States in Gary's footsteps, talking to people who had been close to him, I learned that Bill was not the only one to have seen him again, after his death. I believe it would be unjust and superficial to discard these phenomena as hallucinations. If one of his friends believes he has seen Gary after his death, it must mean that Gary wanted to tell him something very important, and it therefore becomes irrelevant to investigate the event itself - whether it was a dream, a hallucination or a genuine apparition. If someone is convinced that they have seen Gary's spirit, and that Gary has told them something important, it is quite possible that while he was alive Gary had tried to communicate with this person, but they had not realised or understood. Gary's words became much clearer, however, after his death and it is probable that this revelation was so intense that they believed Gary had come to talk to them in person.

Bill's account is of primary importance if we are to understand what happened that night. Gary talked to him of the ´mess´ he had left behind in Europe, Denver and Africa. And he said that he felt relieved to be rid of his body. It is true that Gary was weighed down by a triple failure: one in Europe (his feelings of guilt towards Claude and his son); one in Denver (his inability to ´save´ his friend from disability); and one in Africa, because he had heard that Françoise was with someone else. Gary felt that he was entering another doomed relationship like the one he had suffered with Marie, and maybe this was too much for him to bear. He found it very difficult to accept that he had been wrong about Françoise, had written to her and was waiting for a reply which would prove that, despite her behaviour in Africa, she remained the ideal woman he had believed her to be. But her reply did not arrive. Gary had been to the Post Office that very day and not found the awaited letter.

Gary had talked about all these things with Muffy. Probably he had also discussed them with Bill: and so it is not important if this was when he was alive or dead. Most important was that Bill realised that Gary was extremely tense, and therefore it is not surprising that he felt no pain at losing his friend, when he knew that death had lifted an enormous weight from his shoulders.

CHAPTER TWENTY-THREE

Breaking Point

The coroner's verdict was suicide. Someone notified Gary's mother, and only she attended the funeral - this is strange, but maybe his friends felt a need to distance themselves from his tragic death.

Gary's mother arrived alone from Hawaii. Her husband was in hospital, eventually to die there a few years later. She arrived alone, and alone she followed the coffin to the cemetery. She had not wanted to see the body, and apparently no one had since it had been moved from where it had been found the morning after the tea party. Twenty years later, Lauren, Gary's son, met some hippies in San Francisco - there were still hippies in San Francisco at the end of the 80s - who had never met Gary but had heard much about him. They told Lauren (without knowing who he was) that Gary Hemming was still alive, and claimed that Gary had taken advantage of a stranger's accidental death in 1969 on Lake Jenny to fake his own suicide. He had allowed people to assume that the body was his, and had disappeared finally to fulfil his wish for total freedom, walking over all the mountains in the world. Mythical characters do not die. But in contradiction to the myth, there is the concrete fact of the police report which tells of Gary Hemming killed by a bullet to his head. Suicide or accident? Today, after so many years, it is impossible to find definite proof for either theory.

Gary Hemming had extraordinary qualities, but suffered from contrasting moods which prevented him from developing and cultivating his qualities. He was sociable, he loved being with people and was constantly searching for approval. On the other hand, he lived in deep fear of men and had a love-hate relationship with women. These feelings drove him at times to despise contact with other human beings and to isolate himself for long periods of time. He had ingenious theories, was sharply intuitive and was able to communicate his ideas to others, and persuade them to follow him; but some form of mental indolence would often pervade him and would prevent him from realising a large number of his projects. He felt a need for cleanliness, sincerity, purity and pursued grand ideals - although his behaviour towards his friends and family was often inconsiderate and selfish. All these contradictions weighed heavily on Gary's mind and can maybe explain his emotional instability and changing moods - from the heights of happiness to the depths of despair.

During his life he felt the need for wholeness: he was constantly searching for spiritual equilibrium.

The only field in which Gary succeeded in finding the right balance was in climbing. This is why, while trying to recount the life of a man in all its complexity (there is no alpinist, savant or artist who is not essentially a man made up of virtues and weaknesses), I have talked of Gary first and foremost as an alpinist. When climbing, Gary was able to make use of those extraordinary qualities which he squandered so readily at other times. When climbing he was able to realise his dreams, which left consequences, left their mark.

He took his own life, maybe, because in all the other facets of his life, he was not able to reach that perfect balance, and because the sum of his failures became too great a burden to bear. The version of his death which claims it was accidental does not seem valid; and even if it were true, it would not change anything. Gary had wished for death for some time, and he took his own life that night because the burdens and tensions he suffered from reached breaking point. Whether Gary shot himself or unconsciously brought about a situation which would result in an accident is essentially unimportant and makes no difference to Gary's inevitable fate.

One other theory, however, is feasible: Gary wanted to kill himself but had left the decision to fate and simply lost in a game of Russian roulette. This possibility provides some comfort to those who loved him and who cannot bear the thought of him taking his own life, intentionally and consciously. It is possible that Gary decided to tempt fate, playing a game where the protagonists were his life on the one hand and the intervention of his destiny on the other; hoping that this game would save him, rid him of his problems and restore his confidence in himself, in love and happiness. He had already climbed solo in this very spirit of mind.

And there is one more theory, the one favoured by the European climbing milieu when they heard of Gary's death: he took his own life while experiencing some drug-induced hallucination. Naturally, this theory can neither be confirmed nor denied. Gary went off by himself, and it is possible that he had some form of drug with him so he could go on one of his trips to relieve his tension. But if this was the case, what does it change? Even then, the acid did not kill him, but his own wish for death which pushed him into taking the drugs. After all, Gary was convinced of one thing and that was that no one died by accident or illness, but by a conscious choice, or an unconscious desire to self-destruct.

Long before his death, Gary had overcome the fear of dying and, as early as 1963 he wrote in his diary: "I am sure that the fear of death comes only from the lack of preparation of the person. He doesn't as much fear death as he fears his disorientation in life. A man is capable of facing death easily if he is confident of his own position with respect to the cosmos."

Despite the constant contradictions within his character, Gary had always been sure of his place in the cosmos, his own role. Jokingly his friends would say that he had the nature of a saviour and a hero, and they were right. Gary attached great importance to his role as a saviour, even when this emerged in ridiculous battles, such as his fight to save Marie from her parents. Regardless of the target, he would invest a great deal of energy in carrying out his purpose. Barry Corbet was not in the least surprised when Gary arrived at his house, determined to heal him: he let Gary's magical forces take over, and the experiment failed only because it was physically impossible.

And as for Gary's role as a hero, it fitted him like a glove. Gary was a hero, a hero of his time, in which he represented both good and bad sides. And heroes, of course, die young. Throughout all time, within all cultures, a hero's death is necessary to vindicate his sins and those of others. Maybe Gary, in his heart of hearts, knew that he was a hero who would die young, and he simply followed his fate.

Acknowledgements

This book would not have been possible without the help of those who knew Gary and who agreed to talk to me about him. The list of their names is too long to add here, but they all receive my sincere thanks. Many of them are mentioned in the book, others are not as the length I had decided on did not allow me to include all the anecdotes and accounts I gathered. But those who are not mentioned in the book should know that their contributions were of great value, and by no means superfluous. I would never have been able to get a full picture of Gary's life and of his death without looking at all the details, sometimes minuscule, which have been brought to my attention.

I want to thank most of all those who were close to Gary, who could justifiably have been distrustful of a stranger who wanted to take hold of a part of their personal and family life, but who despite this gave me their trust and their encouragement. Thank you Claude, thank you Lauren.

I owe a sincere apology to Carmen, because I know she will not like this book, but in knowing this I wrote it. I would like her only to read the first chapter and remember that the American Alpine Club awarded her son·a medal of honour for his rescue of the two Germans on the Dru. I would also like her to remember that Gary always carried a Bible with him, the one that she had given to him. These details emerged during my research and I hope that Gary's mother can find some comfort in them.

Some people were of particular assistance, and their contribution was very important: Ken Wilson helped me at the very start when I did not know which direction to take; Tom and Dorene Frost helped me to find important documents and gave me constant encouragement; my conversations with Royal Robbins were enlightening; Barry Corbet helped me to resolve my doubts; Bill Briggs helped me get so close to Gary that I felt I knew him personally.

Thank you, thank you everyone.

And I owe my sincere thanks to Pierre Joffroy who was the great director of my research. He made me work very hard, but it was all worthwhile. Without his help this book would not have been possible. A thank you also to René Desmaison: if he had not introduced me to Pierre Joffroy, it is quite probable that the deus ex machina of my research would never have listened to some stranger who had got it into her head to write the biography of his friend. Thanks to Pierre Mazeaud: he was right, for those who knew Gary well, their life takes on a greater depth. Thanks to Lothar Mauch, Gilles Bodin and all the friends from Chamonix. Thanks to Jerry Gallwas, who suddenly turned up one day with precious information and then as suddenly disappeared again; and thanks to Carlos, Pete, Sterling, Peggy, Muffy and all Gary's friends whom I met in California, Wyoming and Colorado.

Thank you to Carlo Graffigna, to Franco Gaudiano and to Enrico Camanni for their patient reading and constructive comments.

And finally I send my thanks to my husband, Luciano Tenderini, who inspired me to take on this task and who helped with the final version with suggestions and observations. This book is dedicated to him.

M.T.
January 1990

BIBLIOGRAPHY

Allsop K., *Hard Travellin' - The Hobo and his history.*
London 1967

Bonatti W., *On the Heights.* London 1964

Cappon M., *L'Alpinismo.* Milan 1981

Cassarå E., *La Morte del chiodo.* Bologna 1983

Desmaison R., *Total Alpinism.* London 1982

Devies L., Henry P., *Guide Vallot de la Chaîne du Mont Blanc.*
Paris 1967

Gillman P., Haston D., *Eiger Direct.* London 1966

Joffroy P., *Les petits chemins de l'abîme.* Paris 1980

Karl R., *Yosemite.* Bad Homburg 1982

Labande F., *Grandes courses.* Paris 1980

Magnone, G., *West Face.* London 1955

Mazeaud P., *Naked before the Mountain.* London 1974

Meyers G., *Yosemite Climber.* London-Modesto 1979

Michel A., Clébert J-P., *Légendes et traditions de France.*
Paris 1979

Ortenburger L., *A Climbers' Guide to the Teton Range.*
Palo Alto 1979

Rébuffat G., *Le Massif du Mont Blanc.* Paris 1974

Roper S., Steck A., *Fifty Classic Climbs of North America.*
London-San Francisco 1979

Rowell G A., *Yosemite.* Berkeley 1973

Salter J., *Solo Faces.* Boston 1979

Scott D., *Big Wall Climbing.* London 1973

Sinclair P., *We Aspired: the last innocent Americans.*
Ohio 1992

Ullman J R., *Straight Up: John Harlin - the life and death of a mountaineer.* New York 1968

FROM JOURNALS AND MAGAZINES

La Montagne et Alpinisme. October 1964. Gareth Hemming in
        collaboration with Claude Guerre-Genton. *A la
reserche d'un équilibre.*
Le Dauphiné Libéré. August 18th to 23rd inc. 1966.
Paris Match. August 1966. R Desmaison. *Ma place était
la-haut.*
Paris Match. August 1966. Pierre Joffroy. *Dans la tourmente
du Dru, un héros est né.*

Elle. October 13th 1966. Marie-Françoise Leclerc , " Gary Hem-
ming repond a 35 questions qui vont tres loin".
Paris-Match, no. 1064, August 1969: Pierre Joffroy, "Gary Hem-
ming, la fin tragique d'un poete".
La Rivista della Montagna, July 1983: Enrico Camanni, Andrea
Gobetti, "L'utopia oltre le montagne".
Montagnes Magazine, July 1986: Christine Grosjean, "L'Hotel de
tous les paris".
La Montagne et l'Alpinisme, October 1969: René Desmaison,
"Gary Hemming", (obituary).
Mountain Magazine, November 1969: Royal Robbins, "Gary
Hemming", (obituary).

Published in various American magazines, various dates:
Royal Robbins, "Americans in the Alps".
X., " A Tribute to American Climbers".
Tom Frost, "En faisant le fou".
John Harlin, "First Ascents in the Mont Blanc Alps".
Jeremy Bernstein, "En vous recherche".
Royal Robbins, "In Memory of Gary Hemming" (obituary).
Henry W. Kendall, "Gareth H. Hemming" (obituary).

INDEX

188